A Far Cry From Noah

A Far Cry
From Noah

by

Peter Stevenson
POLITICAL AND LEGAL DIRECTOR OF
COMPASSION IN WORLD FARMING

GREEN PRINT
LONDON

First published in 1994 by
Green Print
an imprint of The Merlin Press Ltd
10 Malden Road, London NW5 3HR

ISBN 1 85425 089 2

Printed in the EC by The Cromwell Press

For Annie

and Ruaridh

and Peter Roberts, founder of Compassion in World Farming, who for many years worked with great devotion on the campaign to end the export of live farm animals and who kindly gave me access to all his files and notes

and with thanks to Molly, who typed this book with her usual patience, good humour and warmth.

Contents

Foreword by Joanna Lumley
Introduction

Part One: The History of the Live Trade

Part Two: The Live Trade Today

Part Three: The Way Forward

Foreword

by Joanna Lumley

Humanity has over the centuries shown a notorious predilection for inflicting pain and suffering on the weak – both of its own species and others.

Here is the sad story of a modern betrayal: the story of how a system of free trade took precedence over compassion; of how our nation, and others, systematically subjected farm animals to horrendous suffering en route to vile deaths. It's a tale of tiny calves, torn from their mothers and shunted from one country to another to face a life of solitary confinement and immobilisation; a tale of young lambs snatched from green fields and moist hillsides to dehydrating and stressful journeys in overcrowded trucks going from country to country, only to end up at slaughterhouses where animal welfare is an unknown concept.

Philosophers may indulge in endless debate about whether animals have rights. Most of us would agree that at least they have a right to a decent quality of life and to be slaughtered as painlessly as possible.

But surely the vital question is – what right do we humans have to exploit animals like this? Surely just being the stronger, more technologically developed species confers no intrinsic right to prey on weaker creatures? Can it be that farmers, exporters, and haulage contractors have a right to make rich pickings – no matter what the suffering of the animals involved? No? Then can the God of free trade be justification in itself?

Because as soon as one protests at the horrors of the live export trade one comes up against official Ministry of

Agriculture cop-out-speak – 'our hands are tied' ... 'we cannot ban the trade because of the European treaties' ... 'we would be taken to the European court' ...

Peter Stevenson has done an excellent job investigating this disgusting trade in misery. Compassion in World Farming has worked tirelessly to highlight the suffering inherent in the live export trade. I can only hope this book will help achieve that change of heart which is so badly needed in our bureaucracy and government. Indeed one is led to wonder if governments which allow such cruelties have 'heart' at all?

We proudly regard ourselves as animal lovers – we believe that Britain leads the way in Europe on animal welfare. How wrong we've been. Any country that complacently exports thousands of animals a day to a fate worse than death – but often including death – deserves no accolades.

A Far Cry From Noah truly lives up to its title. My hope is that it will activate and motivate as many people as possible so that our government is forced to listen to our demands for an end to this intolerable trade in living creatures. As long as we do nothing, the suffering will continue. So I urge you all to read this essential story. Read it, rage, repent ... but above all, read it.

Introduction

Noah's ark. The first recorded instance of animal transport. Its purpose was benign. To save the creatures of the earth from the impending flood. Throughout its course they were cared for and nourished.

Nowadays animals are transported not for their benefit but for ours. Crammed into livestock trucks, they are hauled huge distances across Europe without food, water or rest. They arrive battered and bruised. Some do not survive the journey. Their well-being is given scant importance. Governments mouth the right words about welfare, but those words are empty of commitment and action.

And yet this need not be. It certainly should not be. In the Old Testament story at the end of the flood God established the covenant of the ark. This was not just with Noah but with the fowl, the cattle and the beasts.

'I will remember my covenant', said God, 'which is between me and you and every living creature of all flesh'. We, however, seem to have lost sight of our side of the bargain, and daily inflict great suffering on other living creatures. We have indeed come a long way from Noah.

Part One

The History of the Live Trade

Chapter One

Early Days

The export of live farm animals – sheep, lambs, cattle, pigs – is increasingly condemned by the public. Yet the trend is for things to get worse. Each year ever more animals are exported; each year they travel ever greater distances. In 1963 the UK exported some 655,000 live animals. Thirty years on in 1993 that figure rose to 2.5 million.

The modern trade in the export of live animals for slaughter began in 1956 with cattle. American servicemen stationed in continental Europe were hungry for meat and looked to Britain for supplies of beef. Unfortunately British slaughter-houses failed to come up to the standards set by the American Army Veterinary Corps. And so the trade began. Live cattle were shipped abroad to fulfil an American Army contract with the animals being slaughtered in Dutch abattoirs which had been approved by the American authorities.

Soon the Dutch civilian trade became aware of the availability of high quality British cattle and, as a result, they joined the American Army in importing live animals. French buyers then got wind of this development and bought British cattle in Rotterdam.

The facts behind this new trade quickly leaked out. The majority of the cattle sent abroad were old cows, worn-out after years of supplying calves and milk. Others were pregnant or in-milk. All animals quite unsuited to withstand the rigours of long journeys.

One body that was active very early on was the Protection of Livestock for Slaughter Association. They told of nightmare journeys in sealed trucks and storm-battered voyages in the cramped holds of ships. Cows died from thirst and exhaustion. One eye-witness reported:

> I followed a consignment of 100 animals from Britain to an abattoir in France. None received either food or water for five days. The cows were left for 48 hours before slaughter in open pens suffering terribly in paralysing cold.[1]

Some cattle were sent as far afield as Italy. The public was particularly shocked to learn that many of the exported cattle were slaughtered with the pole-axe, a system so cruel that it had been outlawed in Britain since 1933.

The Balfour Report

Faced by mounting public concern, the government did what governments always do in such situations: it set up a Committee of Enquiry. The Balfour Committee's report was published in April 1957 and stated:

> Slaughter before export would be desirable.[2]

In so saying, they struck a note which has been at the core of the debate ever since. For almost four decades it has been argued that the export of live farm animals is largely a totally unnecessary trade.

The majority of the animals will be slaughtered on, or soon after, arrival at their destination. Animals should not be subjected to the stress and suffering of long journeys, only for them to be slaughtered at the journey's end. Instead, they should be killed near the farm on which they have been reared, with the carcases being exported. Put simply, unlike live animals, meat cannot suffer from being transported.

Unfortunately the Balfour Committee shrank from recommending an end to the live trade. Instead it insisted that live animals should only be exported from the UK to countries willing to give the following 'Balfour Assurances':

1. Animals must not travel more than 100 kilometres (62 miles)

from the port where they land in Europe to the slaughter-house.

2. Importing countries must not re-export UK animals.

3. Animals must be stunned before slaughter either by a captive bolt pistol or by electrical stunning.

4. Animals must be properly fed and watered while awaiting slaughter.

One point that emerged from the Balfour Report was the role of the British taxpayer in subsidising live exports. Subsidies and grants were paid to British farmers to encourage them to produce more meat for home consumption. In fact though, some of those subsidies were being paid out for animals which were then sent abroad to benefit European consumers. Not for the last time public monies were being used to subsidise a trade condemned as unethical by the public.

Growing Opposition

Initially many were reassured by the Balfour Assurances, believing them to be effective. In 1963, however, there were reports of the terrible sufferings of sheep on long journeys across Europe and on to North Africa. Under pressure from the public, the Balfour Assurances, which originally only applied to cattle, were extended to sheep and pigs in 1964.

In view of the national disquiet, Mr Denys Bullard MP, himself a Norfolk farmer, introduced a Private Member's Bill to prohibit the export of farm animals for slaughter. In his speech to the House of Commons on 22nd April 1964, he said:

I hold strongly to the principle that animals should be slaughtered as near home as possible without unnecessary long journeys . . .. I am a livestock farmer and I have framed the Bill out of a wish to do the right thing by these animals.

A Private Member's Bill is one introduced by an individual MP rather than by the government. The procedure for such a

Bill is somewhat bizarre and often any MP can kill a Bill by calling out one word, 'Object'. Sadly, Mr. Bullard's humane reform was destroyed by this simple expedient.

1964 did, however, see one beneficial development. The Exported Animals Protection Order 1964 stipulated that, before being loaded on board ship, any cattle, sheep or pigs being exported had to be given food, water and at least ten hours rest at an approved port lairage. (A lairage is simply a place where animals can lie down and be given food and water.)

This new law also stipulated that before loading animals had to be examined by a vet and certified as fit to be shipped. This mandatory lairaging at the ports served animals well until it was swept away by an EC Directive in 1993. The Eurocrats, blind to any consideration other than freedom of trade, judged this minimal tending of livestock at the Channel ports to be 'in restraint of trade'.

In 1965 a fresh spotlight was thrown on the trade by a leading article in *The Veterinary Record*, the official journal of the British Veterinary Association. The Record observed:

> existing knowledge of animal psychology, incomplete though it is, makes it certain that the transport of livestock by road or rail, followed by loading into ships, the unloading, and further transport to a different place of slaughter can hardly be justified, to say the least, in terms of humanity ... it is our duty to say that such traffic should stop.

Given this clear condemnation of the trade by the veterinary profession, one may ask why this trade continues until this day, and thrives.

Indeed, the Rt. Hon. Christopher Soames MP (then Minister of Agriculture) said, on 11th May 1964, in the House of Commons:

> Undoubtedly, the best way, from all points of view, of exporting meat is in carcase form and the trend from live

exports towards that is what the government hopes to see develop as far as possible, and as soon as possible.

It is somewhat disheartening to find, twenty nine years on, his son the Hon. Nicholas Soames (Parliamentary Secretary at the Ministry of Agriculture) praising the live trade for its contribution to the British economy.

On 24th June 1966 an earlier Parliamentary Secretary, Mr John Mackie MP conceded in the House of Commons that 'Her Majesty's government simply have no jurisdiction over what happens to animals on the other side'. This was an admission not that the government's writ failed to run in the hereafter, but simply that the government had no power to safeguard British animals once they left our shores. It is this very fact that has continued to this day to fuel calls for the export of live animals to be replaced by a carcase trade.

A second attempt to ban live exports was made in a Bill introduced in August 1966 by Mr Michael Clark Hutchison MP. He too failed.

And so the trade was free to continue and grow. Fortunately the public's conscience was not stilled and the trade attracted ever more criticisms in the late 1960's and early 70's.

Economic factors

The unwitting role of the taxpayer in subsidising this trade has already been noted. Consider now this further absurdity. One line of trucks leaves the UK carrying live animals earmarked to feed our continental neighbours, while in the opposite direction approaches another line of trucks bringing meat from abroad for UK consumption.

In 1965 the cost of importing 'meat and meat preparations' amounted to £367,829,000 – over £1 million each day. And at the same time as we were importing these vast mountains of meat, we were sending live animals for slaughter abroad.

Chapter Two

The Pretence of Protection: 1967–1970

Evidence that came to light during the late 1960s and early 1970s made it clear the Balfour Assurances were often being ignored and were, as a consequence, largely ineffective in protecting animals exported from the UK.

Only Belgium, Holland, Italy and West Germany had agreed to the Assurances. France had also agreed but only in respect of cattle; it had refused to give the Assurances for sheep and pigs. Yet, as will be seen later, UK animals were being sent much further afield than just these five countries.

The Assurances, moreover, were not legally binding. They were simply a 'gentleman's agreement'. No enforcement proceedings could be taken when they were broken.

The majority of animals exported were, and still are, being sent abroad for one of two reasons: either for immediate slaughter or for further fattening before slaughter. A third weakness of the Assurances lay in the fact that they only applied to animals destined for slaughter. An exporter could easily evade the Assurances by claiming that his animals were for further fattening. In fact, they may have been sent to a farm abroad for as little as 48 hours before being slaughtered, but as animals destined for further fattening they would have fallen outside the 'protection' of the Assurances.

Indeed, in 1972 the RSPCA claimed that, judging from the returns of the Department of Trade and Industry, only some 20% of animals going abroad were given any protection under the Balfour Assurances.[1]

Sheep, Pigs and Cattle covered by the Agreement

Cattle only covered by the Agreement

Holland

Belgium

W. Germany

France

Italy

The Balfour Assurances

Export of calves

In 1967 traders broke new ground by exporting calves from the dairy herd to Belgium. Between August 1968 and April 1969 the total number of calves exported to the continent was about 25,000.[2] For the period between August 1969 and July 1970 the figure was 35,000.[3]

This trade quickly attracted a storm of protest. The public objected to the stresses of the long journeys, which were often aggravated by hunger, thirst and brutal handling.

People were also appalled by the fact that the majority of these young animals were destined for rearing in veal crates, a system widely judged to be cruel in this country. The veal crate is a tiny, solid-sided wooden box. It is so narrow that from the age of about 2 weeks, the calf cannot turn round. As it gets older it cannot even lie down in a normal stretched-out position.

The calves were mainly being sent to Belgium, Holland and Italy, with smaller numbers going to the Canary Islands and Greece. As animals going for further fattening they were not covered by the Balfour Assurances.

It is sad to note that while the export of 25,000 calves in 1969 attracted widespread public outrage, the principal development since then is that by 1993 the number of calves exported per annum had grown to 450,000. In 24 years the trade had increased eighteen-fold.

The suffering imposed by live exports

The fundamental reason why the live trade has attracted such forceful criticisms for so many years is that long journeys impose unacceptable stress on many of the animals involved.

Animals being transported over long distances may suffer in a variety of ways. They are frequently given neither food nor water, even during journeys of 40 hours or more. Overcrowding is commonplace with animals crammed tightly into lorries with no regard for their space needs. Some are injured during loading, others in the course of their journey.

Loading and unloading are particularly stressful and the situation will be made worse by animals being pushed, shoved and beaten when they do not straight away do what is wanted of them. Drivers require neither training nor licensing. Even simple precautions may be ignored; corners may be taken too fast and brakes applied too sharply, with animals being jolted and thrown around.

The combination of high summer temperatures and poor ventilation in trucks or on board ships has led to great hardship with, in the worst cases, animals dying of suffocation.

In short, the trade is opposed by many because on a day-to-day level it imposes regular stress and suffering on animals. It is, however, in the nature of things that often it is the occasional dramatic disaster that brings the trade to the attention of the public at large and leads to mass calls for live exports to be banned. One such disaster occurred in 1969.

Calves' death on Channel ferry

This accident was first brought to light by Mrs Eileen Bezet of the Dartmoor Livestock Protection Society. For very many years, Mrs Bezet put in an enormous amount of work to expose the facts behind the live trade.

During the night of 25/26th November 1969, 26 out of 128 calves died on board the M.V. *Dragon* which was making the journey from Southampton to Le Havre. The animals died when their two-tier lorry overturned in a Force 8 gale. There was a four hour delay before access could be made to the animals, who, in the opinion of the French vet who examined them, died of suffocation.

One particularly disturbing aspect of this case was that the M.V. *Dragon* put to sea with young calves on board despite the fact that the Meteorological Office had issued a gale warning at 17.57 on 25th November.

The calves' death was raised in a House of Lords debate on 10th March 1970. Lord Conesford suggested that, if animals can be put to sea in spite of gale warnings of Force 8 winds, the law needs to be strengthened. Baroness Stocks asked the government to consider whether the time had not come to suspend the export traffic in live animals. Replying for the government, Lord Beswick said 'I should not have thought that there was any ground at all for suspension'.

Calf exports: farmers' response

Farmers were by no means universally delighted by the trade in young dairy calves. Dairy farmers naturally welcomed the fact that market prices for calves were being pushed up under pressure from export buying.

Beef fatteners, however, were having to pay more for calves and claimed that, at a time of domestic shortages, Britain was exporting the raw material of her own beef industry. Indeed, in 1971, Northern Ireland put a complete embargo on the export of calves 'in the interests of the national economy'. For the same reason the Republic of Ireland prohibited the export of cattle weighing less than 8 cwt. In Britain the Ministry of Agriculture sought to restrict the number of calves being exported through a licensing system. The purpose of the restrictions, said the Ministry, was to ensure that the level of calf exports did not adversely affect the expansion of supplies of home-produced beef.[4]

The National Farmers' Union (NFU), however, said that they would not like to see any interference with the export of calves. In the House of Lords debate of 10th March 1970, Viscount Monckton of Brenchley said:

> many of us who are farmers look for our profit in the export of young calves; and provided they are well looked after, four-day-old calves do not require watering or feeding during the journey.

Cherchez le profit-motive.

Balfour Assurances ignored

From 1970 onwards, evidence came in thick and fast of the suffering involved in the live trade and of frequent breaches of the Balfour Assurances.

In October 1970, an RSPCA team followed a shipment of calves being sent to Belgium for further fattening. The animals crossed from Dover to Ostend in extremely bad weather conditions (severe gale 9 gusting to Force 10).[5]

At that time, British regulations prohibited the export of calves weighing less than 110 lbs. The investigators found that all the animals were below this minimum weight with many weighing less than 90 lbs.

The calves were trailed from Ostend to Weelde by the Dutch border, a distance of some 164 miles. Enquiries suggested that many of the calves stayed only for a short time in Belgium before being sent on to other countries, particularly Italy.

Worse was to follow. The investigation team returned to the coast and watched the unloading of calves which had been shipped aboard the M.V. *Bontekoe* from Sheerness to Zeebrugge.

In the early hours of the morning the calves were driven 186 km. (Balfour limit 100 km.) to the village of Putte near the German border. They were then herded into the local slaughterhouse where they were stunned by being hit over the head with a carpenter's claw hammer.

Then the RSPCA report tells us that:

The calves were crowded into a killing pen about 6ft. by 12ft, one end of which was the bleeding area. When a calf had been stunned, it was shackled to the hoist and dragged through other living calves which were actually sometimes thrown into the blood bath by the unconscious calf on its way up to the hoist.

The calves were all killed within sight of each other. Two feet from them they could see their fellows' throats being cut. They could also see the pile of decapitated heads in one corner. The floors and walls were covered with blood.

Chapter Three

The Evidence Thickens: 1971–1972

Transport in small boats

Some animals being exported were transported in lorries (usually two tier) which crossed the Channel and North Sea on roll-on/roll-off ferries. Others were crammed into the holds of small foreign coasters, often on charter to British exporters. Voyages could take up to twelve days going to parts of North Africa.

Mrs Eileen Bezet told of the cruelty to livestock in these small boats – overcrowding, sailing in gales, brutality during loading.[1] In January 1972 she watched the loading of a small foreign vessel in Dover. She described how 'hundreds of sheep were, as a matter of routine, violently welted across the face with heavy sticks and kicked down the steep gangway by the ship's crew'.

The dangers of sea transport were vividly highlighted in October 1970. 262 Irish cattle left Londonderry bound for the Clyde in a Dutch coaster, the *Hereford Express*. The vessel ran aground in heavy weather off the Mull of Kintyre.

She ended up with seven feet of water in her lower holds, where about 140 of the cattle drowned. The rest had to be destroyed after a rescue attempt was frustrated by gales.[2]

An eyewitness said: 'I have never seen anything like it before. Heavy steel pens had been crushed by the frightened beasts and many animals were lying about injured.'[3] The Daily Telegraph reported that over half the surviving animals were destroyed by RSPCA officers 'but about 50 others, crazed by fear, had broken loose and had to be destroyed by a rifleman'.[4]

Landing

Appalling conditions awaited animals once they landed. Often they would be left waiting at the docks for a considerable time before being taken on the next stage of their journey. Mrs Bezet described how she came across a consignment of British cull cows waiting in the blazing sun at Ostend Docks. The animals were being 'dried out' (denied water) before slaughter. They were making vain attempts to break out of their crammed pens so as to reach water in the adjoining canal. Water containers in the pens were deliberately kept empty.

In February 1970, Mrs Bezet watched British sheep being unloaded in Ostend:

> Handling was rough to the point of brutality; many sheep were lame and in poor condition – some had blood on them. Weak and infirm animals were hurled bodily up the ramp.[5]

Economic implications

As the cruelty involved in the trade became more apparent, so too it became clear that live exports were not necessarily an economic blessing for this country.

Indeed it was argued by some that there were strong economic advantages to slaughtering and processing animals in the UK, and for meeting the overseas demand for British meat by exporting carcases rather than live animals.[6]

In 1972 there were about 40 slaughterhouses in this country approved for the export of meat to the EEC (of which the UK was not yet a member). However, because animals were being sent abroad for slaughter, these British slaughterhouses were being severely under-used. Manchester abattoir, for example, was working at only 50% capacity and in 1971 cost the ratepayers more than £350,000 in operating losses.[7] Most public slaughterhouses (in those days many slaughterhouses were still run by the local authorities) operated at a loss, having to be subsidised by the ratepayers.[8] Many of these losses could have been prevented by slaughtering animals in the UK.

There was also the question of employment. If the exported animals had been killed here, more jobs would have been created in UK slaughterhouses.

Moreover, when live animals were exported, the UK lost not only the animals but also certain by-products, such as hides, skins, offal and slaughtering residuals which were turned into animal feed and fertiliser. The retention in this country of these by-products would have boosted UK processing industries and provided further job opportunities.

Much was made of the fact that live exports brought in foreign currency and made a valuable contribution to the balance of payments. This ignored the fact that the UK consumes much more meat than it produces.

As a result, the UK imports large quantities of meat and meat products – in 1972 over £1,125,000 was spent each day on such imports. Every pound of meat exported, alive or dead, had to be replaced by imports. The export of live animals clearly made no economic sense.

In 1971 the RSPCA and the Sunday Times Insight team revealed how an Irish connection was costing the British taxpayer some £100,000.[9, 10] In 1970, dealers in the Irish Republic signed a contract to supply £1,000,000 of live cattle to North Africa. Investigators began to wonder whether, given the size of the deal, all the animals were being supplied from the Republic. Perhaps, they thought, some were coming from Northern Ireland.

And if they were? What was wrong with that?

Two things. It broke the spirit of the Balfour Assurances and it cost the British taxpayer a small fortune.

Northern Ireland, as part of the UK, could not export animals to a country which was not a party to the Balfour Assurances and no North African country had signed these Assurances.

There was a loophole, however. The Irish Republic had never been asked to sign the Assurances and yet, despite this, the UK exported live animals to the Republic.

In March 1971, the investigation team went to Greenore, a small port just inside the Republic. The border with Northern Ireland is just a mile or two away. Here in Greenore the team witnessed cattle being loaded on board the MV *Shorthorn Express* bound for Tunis and Tripoli.

The investigators knew the cattle were from the North because their ears were punched. Fattening cattle in the UK were eligible for a subsidy and, on payment of the subsidy, their right ears were hole-punched. This subsidy meant that dealers could buy the cattle they needed to fulfil their North African contract at a much cheaper rate in Northern Ireland than in the Republic.

And the subsidy was large – on average one fifth of the animal's value. The purpose of the subsidy was, of course, to provide cheap meat for the UK consumer. It was not designed to provide cheap meat for overseas consumers nor to swell the profit margins of exporters.

A final note. When, after a ten-day sea passage, the cattle arrived, they were driven on foot through Tunis to an abattoir. There they were ritually slaughtered. This means that they were not stunned before slaughter. Instead, the beasts' throats were cut whilst they were fully conscious.

Breach of Assurances: further evidence

In 1972 the RSPCA conducted a detailed probe into the fate of British animals exported to Europe.[11] They found 130 breaches of the Balfour Assurances involving thousands of sheep.[12]

The investigators followed several consignments of British sheep from Ostend to a farm near Wadelincourt near the French border. Enquiries revealed that the farmer regularly re-exported the sheep to France, North Africa and Greece.

Another lorry was followed all the way from Ostend to Marseilles. During the 1240 km. journey the sheep were given neither food nor water. Freshly shorn, they travelled in a semi-open lorry through bitterly cold weather. (Sheep are sometimes shorn shortly before a journey so that more can be crammed on to the lorry.)

The abattoir at Sisteron in Provence slaughtered 8,641 British sheep between 1st January and 6th April 1972.[13] Investigators watched a consignment of 420 being killed:

> They were all 'despatched' by having their throats cut without pre-stunning of any kind. A cut was made in the windpipe about four inches below the angle of the jaw. For this purpose, the animals were held down on their backs. Their necks were bent forward and fastened under a bar – then their throats were completely severed between the angle of the jaw and the slit in the wind-pipe.[14]

The abattoir had electrical stunning equipment but did not use it. Ironically on one wall was a large notice which displayed an order of the French Ministry of Agriculture that it was obligatory to electrically stun animals before slaughter.

This abattoir was not alone in ignoring the law. The French farm animal welfare society Oeuvre d'Assistance Aux Betes d'Abattoirs, run by Madame Jacqueline Gilardoni, produced a shocking report revealing that the French 1964 humane slaughter legislation was widely disregarded. 85% of sheep, 50% of calves and 20% of pigs had their throats cut while fully conscious.

Lest it be thought that only animal welfarists were concerned about conditions in Europe, it is worth reporting that in 1971, during a visit to a well-known Belgian market and abattoir, a party of Welsh butchers, farmers and auctioneers were deeply shocked by the brutal treatment meted out to all classes of stock.[15]

The *Farmers Weekly* account of their visit reports that they thought the brutality involved actually made the job of moving the cattle more difficult. An animal on a halter would be belaboured on the nose by one man in front to slow it down, and driven by another behind to move it forward. As a result, the animals panicked and struggled and so the sticks were wielded more vigorously. The Welsh visitors observed that 'every man in the market carried a stick and was very ready to use it'.[16] In the abattoir they saw bulls with a blindfold of rough sacking being led between the kicking bodies of others, and lambs standing on fleeces and offals to be stunned.

In short, by the end of 1972 there was overwhelming evidence that the Balfour Assurances were being flouted regularly and blatantly. Animals were being transported for well over 100 km; they were frequently being re-exported; and they were often slaughtered without first being stunned.

Despite the mounting evidence of cruelty, the National Farmers Union displayed their customary lack of concern. In 1971 Lord Somers introduced a Bill to prohibit live exports. Shortly before the Bill's Third Reading (its final stage in the House of Lords) the NFU wrote to certain members of the Lords:

> The National Farmers Union it must be repeated are totally opposed to the Bill, and earnestly hope that it will not be given a Third Reading.

At its Third Reading on 17th February 1972, Lord Somers' Bill was duly defeated.

Chapter Four

Government Defeated – Live Exports Stopped

Compassion in World Farming was founded in 1967 to campaign for an end to the factory farming of animals.

In the 1960's, Peter Roberts and his wife Anna were running a small dairy farm in Hampshire. They had always been welfare-minded. Peter recalls how, even in the snow, he would always let his cows out in the morning and they would charge out to the field, muck about for 30–40 minutes and then wander happily back to their clean, straw-bedded cowshed for warmth and comfort.

But there were aspects to farming which made them feel increasingly uneasy. Peter took to going to the slaughterhouse with each cull cow and staying with her until she was dead to make sure that she suffered the minimum of stress. The increasing use of the battery cage for hens also disturbed them greatly. Eventually they became vegetarian and sold their farm, wanting to distance themselves from the cruelties which they now felt were an inherent part of much modern farming.

Shortly afterwards Compassion in World Farming was born and the first newsletter published to oppose the ruthless treatment of farm animals. From an early date Peter Roberts campaigned against live exports.

During the early part of 1973 the pressure from the public for an end to the live trade was becoming unstoppable. In December 1972 Compassion in World Farming had presented to the Minister of Agriculture a petition with over half a million signatures calling for an export ban.

Eventually the cumulative evidence became too much even for the government. On 1st February 1973 the Minister of

Agriculture made an Order suspending the issue of licences for the export of sheep for slaughter or further fattening.

A great victory. Jubilation was, however, tempered by the knowledge that the measure was of a temporary nature rather than a permanent ban on the export of live sheep.

Moreover, the trade in live cattle had not been suspended. The Minister wanted more evidence of cruelty to cattle before he was prepared to act. This was duly produced.

In January and March 1973 the RSPCA and the News of the World published fresh evidence that the cattle trade was bedevilled with infringements of the Balfour Assurances.[1]

Most telling of all was a report published by Maureen Lawless. She told how on Tuesday, 13th March 1973, she saw cattle from Britain being loaded on to two trailers at Ostend:

As the trailers left the dock, we could see cattle lose their footing and fall.

As we pulled alongside the double trailer, one of the beasts fell over and others were thrown on top of him.

Two legs of one steer were sticking through the sides of the trailer and we could see gashes on the legs and heads of many of the animals. But journey's end, at the slaughterhouse in the Belgian village of Izegem, proved even more harrowing.

Workers with sticks and pitchforks beat and prodded the cattle down the ramp and laughed as they slipped or fell.

Terrified and limping, the mass of animals were beaten into a concrete killing area where a man with a pistol aimed haphazardly at them.

Some fell shot in the head. Others not so fortunate were hit in the ear, the cheek or the neck.

The cattle behind tripped over the dead and injured bodies into blood which was inches deep.

One injured beast somehow crawled away and wedged itself under some bars in the corner.

As the shot animals fell or were trying to stagger away, they were hauled up by a chain attached to one hind leg and were left to have their throats cut in full view of the beasts waiting their turn.

One steer with a wound in its cheek was hanging up
by one leg kicking and struggling and bellowing for minutes fully conscious, until one of the men walked over
and actually cut its throat.[2]

The debate in Parliament

The press seemed filled with the debate, with welfarists urg-
ing a ban and farmers insisting their livelihood would be
threatened. On 12th July 1973, the debate spilled over into
Parliament.

The Opposition (Labour) put down a motion calling on the
government to establish an independent inquiry into the
trade, and in the meantime to suspend the issuing of licences
for the export of live animals for slaughter overseas.

During the course of the debate the government announced
that it indeed intended to set up a committee of inquiry. They
refused, however, to accept that in the meantime the trade
should be suspended. Instead they tabled an amendment to
the Opposition motion proposing that the trade should be
stopped only when there was evidence that the Balfour
Assurances were not being kept.

A three hour debate ensued with MPs from all parties calling for live exports to be suspended. The degree of public
anxiety was highlighted by Sir Ronald Russell MP who had
himself brought forward a Bill to ban the trade. He emphasised that he had 'had thousands of letters, petitions and
telephone calls in support of my Bill, and they are still coming'.[3]

Mr F A Burden MP reminded the House that, just two days
before, the British Veterinary Association had sent out a letter
saying:

We do hope that the debate will force a ban on the export
of all live food animals.[4]

The debasing of moral standards inherent in the trade was
stressed by Mrs Sally Oppenheim MP:

We tell our children of the dreadful cruelties perpetrated

against human beings in our earlier history and more recently in Nazi Germany. Then we boast somewhat optimistically about how all this has been changed by progress and civilisation. But how are our children's children to judge us when they read of the degree of cruelty to animals that we were prepared to tolerate and by our own inaction to condone.

Government defeated

At the end of the debate the Minister of Agriculture, the Rt. Hon. Joseph Godber MP, urged the Commons not to vote to suspend the trade.

Amid scenes of great excitement the votes were counted. There were roars of delight when it was announced that the government had been defeated by 285 votes to 264, a majority of 21. The government had been so concerned to ensure the trade's survival that they put considerable pressure on their own (Conservative) MPs to support them. Despite this 23 Tory MPs voted with the Labour Opposition.

The Commons had voted for live exports to be suspended. This must rank as the finest victory in the long fight against live exports.

Live exports suspended

The next day the Minister of Agriculture announced that no new licences would be issued for the export of cattle or pigs (the issue of licences for the export of sheep had already been suspended in February). The government added that they would reconsider the whole question in the light of the report of the independent inquiry.

On July 25th it was announced that the Committee of Inquiry was to be chaired by Lord O'Brien of Lothbury, who had recently retired as Governor of the Bank of England.

Peter Roberts, General Secretary of Compassion in World Farming was quoted in the press as saying:

This decisive defeat for the government has indicated the

strength of feeling not only in the House but in the country. Now we've got to see that all the loopholes are closed.[5]

Economic factors

Before going on to examine the O'Brien Committee's report, it is worth looking at the debate that was taking place on the economic pros and cons of the trade.

Koen Leflere, Sales Manager of the Izegem abattoir exposed earlier in the year, had no doubts:

> We do not want to buy English carcases. We only want your live animals. We are just in this business to make money.[6]

But was the live trade to the UK's benefit? The farming press pointed out that in 1972, the last full year of exports, £20 million-worth of cattle, sheep and pigs had been exported for slaughter.[7] They argued that the suspension of the trade would cost the country £20 million a year.

This argument was far too simplistic and ignored a number of factors. The UK consumes much more meat than it produces. At that time the UK was importing meat to the value of about £500 million a year, some of which was to replace the animals exported alive.

In the context of these massive imports, it can be seen that the £20 million-worth of live exports made no contribution to the UK's adverse balance of payments position. If instead of being sent abroad, those animals had been slaughtered for home consumption, the UK could have reduced its meat imports bill.

This position can be illustrated by looking at cattle. Britain was producing only about 70% of the beef required by the home market. To make up the balance, Britain imported about 400,000 live cattle a year (and over a million beef carcases from the Irish Republic alone). At the same time, however, we exported about 150,000 live cattle each year.[8]

If animals had been slaughtered at home not only would the

UK have been able to reduce its imports bill, but it would also have benefited from what is known as 'added value'. This simply refers to the extra wealth created by slaughtering and processing animals at home.

The Irish Republic was quick to recognise the economic benefits of exporting meat rather than live animals. Mr John O'Callaghan, Chairman of the Fresh Meat Exporters Society in Dublin, said at their 1972 AGM:

> The added value derived from processing each animal in Ireland can be as much as £24. When this is contrasted with the livestock trade, which provides no employment and no added value, there can be no doubt as to which method of handling Ireland's cattle production benefits the country most.[9]

In 1973, the Irish Economic and Social Research Institute published a study of the Irish cattle industry in which they said that, if cattle are slaughtered in the home country, there is a considerable 'value added' by reason of producing the meat and by-products within the country. They estimated that the Irish cattle slaughtering industry generated an annual Gross National Product (GNP) of £12 million over and above the GNP obtained by a similar live export trade. The Irish Livestock and Meat Board accordingly came down heavily in favour of meat exports instead of live exports.

In 1973 the UK exported 153,000 cattle. On the basis of the calculations used by the Irish study, the additional value to the UK balance of payments, had all these animals been slaughtered at home, would have been £2,750,000.[10]

In short, it is clear that the live trade damages the home economy by exporting the UK's raw material which could be used to create extra profit and employment here rather than enriching overseas buyers.

Chapter Five

Resumption of Trade

The O'Brien Report

On 27th March 1974, the O'Brien Committee published its Report.

The Committee concluded that although there had been shortcomings in the operation of the trade, a permanent ban on the export of live animals was not justified either on welfare or economic grounds (para. 21).[1]

In the months that followed, those who wished to see a resumption of the trade often referred to this conclusion, conveniently omitting the second part of paragraph 21 of the Report. This stipulated that the issue of export licences should continue to be suspended until acceptable and enforceable conditions could be introduced to ensure that the welfare of the animals was safeguarded with greater certainty.

The Committee went on to propose a number of safeguards including the establishment of both an export supervisory body and a small team of inspectors to investigate allegations of misconduct (paras. 100–104). The Committee also recommended that exports should be allowed only to approved destinations (para. 105).

The British Veterinary Association (BVA) quickly issued a Press Statement expressing their concern that the Report's proposals did not go far enough and would not be really effective. They stressed that:

The BVA has not changed its view that animals should be slaughtered as near to the place of production as possible.[2]

The animal welfare bodies made it clear that they were deeply disappointed that the Report had not come out against live exports for slaughter. Peter Roberts of Compassion in World Farming condemned it as a restatement of Ministry of Agriculture policy over the last ten years: 'Keep Live Exports Going; Plug The Leaks; Make It Respectable'.[3]

Many had hoped that the Report would have championed the policy that animals destined for slaughter should be killed as near as possible to the farm on which they were reared.[4] Those opposed to the trade felt that the Committee had dealt in a cursory manner with the representations of the animal welfare bodies. Indeed, one MP said that 'all too frequently it [the Report] seems to whitewash existing practices... It abounds in complacency'.[5]

Others pointed out that the Committee's own investigations were deeply flawed. Rather than going incognito, they had given advance notice of their intention to visit various places. If, for example, an abattoir knows it is to be visited by the O'Brien Committee on such and such a date, it will inevitably clean up its act for the day of the visit.

The National Farmers Union welcomed the Report calling it 'objective and constructive'.[6] Not all farmers, however, shared in the general jubilation. Mr McCall-Smith, a sheep and cattle producer, said in his presidential address to the Scottish Peat and Land Development Association:

> There is no excuse for exporting frightened animals to a virtually unknown fate overseas. Public money has been used to produce these animals, for example, a £18 calf subsidy, and they should be sold on the home market.[7]

Since the 1973 debate which had led to the suspension of live exports, there had been a general election and Labour now formed the government. On the Report's publication, the Agriculture Minister, the Rt. Hon. Fred Peart MP, said that he would consider it very carefully but that, in the meantime, the ban on exporting animals for slaughter must stay.[8]

So it was that the Report was not debated by Parliament until 16th January 1975.

Parliament's debate

Labour, which eighteen months before had called loudly for the trade to be suspended, had now changed its tune. The government was proposing to the Commons that live exports should be resumed to other EEC countries 'and to such other countries as can provide adequate safeguards'.[9]

Particularly shocking was the government's proposal that the trade should start up again immediately. This completely ignored the O'Brien Committee's stricture that the trade's suspension should continue until proper safeguards were in place.

Referring to the conditions recommended by O'Brien, the Minister said that all the welfare interests doubted whether they could be enforced in practice. He went on to confess: 'I think they are correct in their assessment'.[10]

Rather than accepting that if the O'Brien safeguards were unworkable the trade should not be resumed, the Minister drew the extraordinary conclusion that the trade could go ahead without even trying to make the safeguards work.

In doing so, the Minister relied heavily on just one aspect of the Report, which had stressed the need for Europe-wide regulations on transport and slaughter.

The Minister pointed with satisfaction to the fact that the EC had adopted a Directive requiring animals to be stunned before slaughter which was due to come into force on 1st July 1975.[11]

A year later one journal mentioning this Directive, commented:

> Unhappily, being bound by a Directive does not automatically mean that it is universally obeyed, and there is no doubt that vigilance is still needed.[12]

This was the view not of a rabid welfarist but of the magazine of the National Farmers Union.

The RSPCA too did not share O'Brien's rosy view of European abattoirs. They said that inhumane slaughter was the rule rather than the exception, and that when their Chief

Veterinary Officer was visiting one French abattoir at least six slaughtermen were cutting animals' throats without pre-stunning.[13] Even today the EC Directive can fail to be an effective safeguard; for example, in 1990 and again in 1991, Compassion in World Farming brought back videos showing sheep being slaughtered in Spain without any attempt at pre-stunning.

Another aspect of slaughter was referred to in paragraph 17 of the O'Brien Report which stated that 'enervation' was permitted in Italy. Surprisingly, the Report made no mention of what enervation is.

The term was explained to the Commons:

> It means that a sharp three-cornered instrument called a puntilla, a small knife with a triangular blade, is inserted into the base of the skull of the animal to sever that part of its spinal rapport responsible for the nerve centres controlling the limbs. The animal is not rendered unconscious. It is immobilised so that it cannot kick the slaughterman when he cuts its throat. It is fully conscious and it has full feeling.[14]

Turning to transport, the Minister pointed to the Council of Europe Convention on the welfare of animals during international transport.[15] In doing so he chose to ignore the cardinal principle set out in the Convention's Explanatory Report that, as regards animals being transported for slaughter:

> the ideal would be to restrict international traffic to carcase meat thus ensuring that the animals were slaughtered in the country of origin.

In fact the Convention has been of very limited value in protecting animals during transport. Much of the Convention and the subsequent EC Directives on transport have been too short on detail and have rarely been enforced in much of the EC. This was conceded in 1993 by the European Commission which accepted that EC rules on feeding and watering are 'systematically flouted'.[16]

One argument deployed during the Commons debate in favour of lifting the suspension was that after a poor summer in 1974, fodder was in short supply that winter. Some farmers ran an 'export them or watch them starve' campaign.

There were indeed fodder shortages in Wales, the South-West and Scotland. It was argued that 'it is far better to send them [cattle] overseas than to allow them to starve on the Welsh hills'.[17]

An opposing view was, however, expressed by the *Farmers Weekly*:

A few cargoes of Belgium-bound cows will cause scarcely an eddy in the flood-stream of stock pouring through UK slaughterhouses. The only way to avert tragedy in the livestock areas of the West is to import more feed, and to see that farmers have the cash to pay for it.[18]

At the end of a seven hour debate, the government had its wicked way, winning by 232 votes to 191.

The export of live animals began once more and has continued unabated ever since. Amidst all the talk of the O'Brien safeguards (largely never implemented), two elements of the erstwhile Balfour Assurances were quietly dropped.

No longer was there to be a 100 km. limit on the journey from the port to the abattoir. Nor was there to be any prohibition on a receiving country re-exporting UK animals. In the 1990s with frequent journeys to the south of France, Italy and Spain, many of us long for the good old days of the 100 km. journey limit.

Chapter Six

And The Trade Goes On: 1975–1982

Once Parliament had given live exports the go-ahead in January 1975, dealers wasted little time in getting the trade back into full swing. Evidence of cruelty and law-breaking followed hard on the heels of the trade's resumption.

In Spring 1975, a *Midweek* television film followed a consignment of British sheep through France. The exporter gave the destination of the animals as Paris. In fact, 48 hours after leaving Dover a lorryload of cold and frightened sheep arrived in the South of France. During the whole 48 hours they had not been given food, water or rest.

On 1st July 1975, the new EEC Directive requiring animals to be humanely stunned before slaughter came into force. In the autumn, Madame Gilardoni, Founder-President of the Oeuvre d'Assistance aux Betes d'Abattoirs disclosed evidence showing that many French slaughterhouses were ignoring this law. For example, in the abattoir at Brive, the OABA found that sheep were bled while conscious and calves were haphazardly struck on the head with a sledgehammer. At Lambelle sheep had their throats cut without first being stunned.[1]

The RSPCA Special Investigations Unit followed sheep transporters on six different occasions in 1977. The animals travelled distances in excess of 1250 km. with one consignment covering 1425 km. The journeys averaged 30 to 37 hours. Numerous consignments of calves were also found to have travelled in excess of 24 hours without nourishment.[2] In one instance, cattle had been carried from Calais to Italy for more than 47 hours without rest, feed or water.[3]

It was this background of continuing neglect and abuse which caused the British Veterinary Association, at its meeting on 29th June 1977, to resolve unanimously that:

> it does not agree with the export of live animals for immediate slaughter and considers that animals should be slaughtered as near the point of production as possible.[4]

In response to growing public unrest the Ministry of Agriculture called for yet another report. This report, produced by a working group of Ministry officials, was published on 23rd March 1978.[5]

The report stated that 'there is ... sufficient evidence from reliable sources to conclude that some consignments of animals have been carried without food or water for periods of time longer than the expert advice would suggest to be reasonable'. Within the crabbed, guarded language of officialdom, they seemed to be admitting that the live trade led to stress and suffering.

The report went on to conclude that 'on the economic aspects ... the weight of advantage to the UK lies in continuing the trade.

Economic aspects

Not surprisingly, the report placed economic gain above the welfare of the animals. Rather more surprisingly, it appeared to ignore a number of compelling arguments suggesting that the live trade was not to the UK's economic advantage.

It was, and still is, often argued that live exports earn the UK valuable foreign currency, and make an important contribution to the country's balance of payments situation. At first sight this is an impressive point, but it does not stand up to close scrutiny.

The UK imports very much more meat than it exports. If the UK refused to export live animals, substantial savings could be made on its imports bill.

For example, in 1977 the UK was spending over £3 million

per day on importing meat and meat products. Yet 169,000 live calves were exported during the first eight months of that year. They fetched £11.5 million. If, however, the calves had stayed in the UK and been fattened, they would have been worth up to £55 million. Put simply, in order to gain £11.5 million of exports, the UK sacrificed the opportunity of reducing its import bill by up to £55 million.[6]

Many farmers benefited from live exports as competition from foreign buyers pushed up prices for cattle and sheep. Slaughterhouse operators and beef farmers, however, were firmly opposed to the live trade. No doubt it came as a surprise to both the slaughterhouses and the welfare bodies to find themselves on the same side of the argument.

Abattoirs are costly places to run both in terms of their capital equipment and their staff. If they do not have enough animals to kill each week, they may make a loss. The export of live animals was proving disastrous, robbing UK abattoirs of the beasts they needed to kill if they were to remain profitable. It is for this reason that the meat trade (as opposed to farmers) continues to this day to oppose live exports.

Beef farmers too were threatened by the live trade. Young calves are their 'raw material', which they rear on until they become full grown cattle. They found that they could not make adequate profit margins as calf prices were being pushed through the roof by competition from European buyers. Moreover, the beef farmers complained that the export trade was creaming off the best of the calves, leaving lower quality animals to be reared at home.[7]

Many of these concerns were voiced by the Farmers Weekly:

> As we export our raw materials – for hide and offal as well as for meat – we ship with it jobs at abattoirs and processing plants ... it is stupid to deprive the home producer of the best raw material and still expect him to turn dear calves into cheap meat.[8]

It should be stressed that there was no technical difficulty in exporting meat rather than live animals. Chiller-lorries were available and chilled meat could safely be transported throughout the EC. It is worth emphasising that it is not necessary to freeze meat for transport within the EC; chilling is sufficient.

Indeed then, as now, the majority of the trade was in meat. In 1981, roughly 1,009,000 sheep carcases were exported compared with 58,000 live sheep. In other words, 95% of the export trade was in animals which had been slaughtered in the UK. To animal welfare bodies it seemed perverse not to convert the whole trade to one in carcases thereby eliminating the stress inherent in long distance transport.

New Directives but no policing

On 1st August 1978, EC Directive 77/489 came into force. This was intended to protect animals during international transport.

In particular, it provided that animals must not travel for longer than 24 hours without being given food and water. This compared unfavourably with UK law (the Transit of Animals (Road and Rail) Order 1975) which required animals to be given food and water every 12 hours.

The 1977 Directive was supplemented by a further EC Directive in 1981 (81/389/EEC). This required each consignment of animals to be accompanied by an international animal transport certificate, which recorded a number of details, including when the animals were loaded and their destination abroad.

These details were intended to aid enforcement by the various EC Member States as vehicles carrying animals passed through their territory.

To officials both in the UK and the EC, these new Directives were a boon. The answer to all complaints was to point to the impressive safeguards provided by the law. The enquirer was dazzled by erudite references to such and such a section and paragraph (x) of sub-clause (y), etc.

All this was purely a paper reality. In most of the EC the

regulations were not policed and breaches of the law were routine.

For example, in June 1981, the RSPCA followed a consignment of calves which received neither food nor water for 30 hours. Also in that year, members of the Dartmoor Livestock Protection Society witnessed calves lifted by their ears and tails in France, and French handlers hitting calves on the nose and tugging them so roughly that they were left with torn ears.[9]

In 1982, a consignment of sheep was followed from the UK to South-West France. Many of them started their journey in Scotland. They crossed from Dover to Calais during a gale.

On Calais docks they were transferred from two British lorries on to a 4-tier French transporter. They were so crowded that the driver had to prod them with a pole to pack them in. They were driven south through the night in torrential rain; the sheep on the lower tiers were drenched, cold and hungry. By morning many were in a state of collapse; one had its front legs broken.

527 miles from Calais they finally arrived at the abattoir at Prudhomat in the Lot departement of France.[10]

Reports such as this continued to shock the public, but the Ministry's only response was to talk soothingly of legal safeguards and thorough investigations. In fact, to talk of anything other than putting an end to the trade.

Chapter Seven

The Same Old Story: 1983–1989

The pattern established since the resumption of trade in 1975 continued throughout the 80's. The live trade continued to thrive, the public continued to protest and officialdom continued to refuse to take effective action.

Sheep, lambs, calves and cattle were packed into trucks and subjected to jolting, noise, fumes, too little food, no water, excessive heat, excessive cold. In short, the universal horror story of international live animal transport.

Formal complaint to European Commission

In 1985, the RSPCA submitted a formal complaint to the European Commission against the UK and French governments.[1] They argued that the UK had failed properly to implement the EC Directive on transport (77/489/EEC) and that France had failed to enforce it.

The complaint centred round reports of 137 trails carried out by the RSPCA. These showed that the Directive was being flouted on a massive scale.

Unbelievably, on only one of the 137 journeys had the driver stopped to give food and water to the animals. So often the cry of authority, on being presented with a fresh horror, is: it's terrible, but it's only an isolated incident, in general the trade conducts itself responsibly. Here was clear evidence that the only 'isolated incident' was when the animals were given food and water. The norm was for the law to be ignored.

The EC Directive required animals to be given food and water at least every 24 hours. The Trail Reports attached to the complaint showed that nearly half of the journeys lasted more than 24 hours and that (with the one shining exception) no food and water stops were made. Some journeys lasted over 30 hours and in one case 48 hours – again with no food or water.

The complaint stressed that:

The system as operated by the UK favours the commercial needs of road hauliers and exporters and disregards the interests of animal welfare.

The Commission upheld the complaint and announced that both the UK and France were to be taken to the European Court of Justice. Before the case could come to Court both the UK and France caved in. The UK undertook to bring in new regulations designed fully to implement the EC Directive. France promised to give a higher profile to enforcement. Needless to say, nothing much changed on the ground. Animals continued to suffer and the law continued to be ignored.

Live exports to Spain

In October 1986, the Observer published a report by Victor Smart who had followed a consignment of 583 British sheep ostensibly bound for France. In fact, they ended up 27 hours later in Northern Spain after a nightmare journey during which 'as they fight for space some animals' legs are forced through the sides of the transporter'.[2]

On arrival at least one was dead and others dying from exhaustion. Some were thrown from the top of the four-deck lorry to the ground.

The animals should never have gone to Spain. The UK government refused to issue licences for animals to be sent for slaughter to Spain as that country had not yet implemented the EC Directive on humane stunning before slaughter.

On 23rd November 1986, the Observer published a further report having followed a load of 489 sheep from the Midlands to Dover and then to France. After 37 hours without food or water the RSPCA intervened.

European Parliament

On 20th January 1987, the European Parliament debated a report by Richard Simmonds MEP on farm animal welfare.

Barbara Castle MEP made a moving contribution to the debate:

> The conditions under which sheep, young calves and other live animals are being carted not only across the water but across the Continent are heartbreaking. Carried without food and water, without proper ventilation, herded together, frightened, trampling each other to death and arriving in a state of intense suffering.

The Parliament voted to adopt the Report by 150 votes with none against. In particular, they voted for an EC Inspectorate to be established to monitor the trade and to investigate infringements of Directives. In 1994 we still await the establishment of a properly funded EC Inspectorate of sufficient size to carry out its work effectively.

The madness goes on

The decade ended as it had begun with the trade in full swing. An exposé in the Sunday Times of 29th October 1989 alleged that sheep were being sent all the way from Scotland to Spain for slaughter.[3]

The Sunday Times told how in October up to 7,000 lambs a day, raised in the north of Scotland, are auctioned at Perth livestock market. In 1989 a Suffolk Cross lamb may have been bought for £40 in Perth but would fetch twice that sum in southern Europe.

TABLE: EXPORT FIGURES FOR 1986 – 1989

	1986	1987	1988	1989
Lambs & sheep	161,762	313,556	446,767	491,892
Calves	190,683	365,166	234,651	302,223

Source: Ministry of Agriculture, Fisheries and Food.

Investigators followed a consignment of 557 British lambs on a 30-hour journey to a staging post near Toulouse in southern France. By law, the journey should have been broken to give the lambs food and water.

The driver did indeed break the journey, but only to give himself a night's sleep. Early the next morning the lambs were driven off – at no stage had they been given either food or water. The lairage owner's wife was quoted as saying 'We'll give documents even if the livestock is not taken off [the lorry]. The price is the same'.

The investigators reported that the sheep were in obvious distress by the time they got to Toulouse. Many had yellow nasal discharge and others were coughing; some died.

At the staging post lambs were mainly being kept in two open concrete pens. The floors comprised loose roadstone, dust and straw. 'I made a mistake building those pens', the owner was quoted as saying. 'I realise now that sheep like grass'.

He went on to claim that only six of 30,000 British lambs had died since the start of his French operation. Minutes later, however, he admitted that several had died that day. 'Three committed suicide', he said, insisting that they fell into a water trough.

According to the export licence, the lambs' final destination was France. However, the Sunday Times alleged that within days of arriving in southern France some of the lambs were sent to a Madrid slaughterhouse. This was in breach of the export licence and in defiance of the UK government's ban on animals being sent to Spain for slaughter.

The live exports statistics for 1989 showed a worrying increase over those for 1988 with over 100,000 more farm animals being exported than in the previous year.

It was clear that standards had fallen dramatically since the UK had joined the European Community on 1st January 1973. Indeed, in Compassion in World Farming's early days, when the UK was about to join what was then called the 'Common Market', Joan Quennell, then MP for Petersfield, presented, at the request of the trustees of Compassion in World Farming, a petition to the House of Commons. This drew attention to the dangers to the UK's animal welfare standards of entering the Common Market as Parliament would lose its freedom to legislate in this field.

In the old days under the Balfour Assurances, journeys were, at least in theory, limited to 62 miles from the port of disembarkation on the Continent to the final abattoir. By 1989 the journeys could stretch to over 1,000 miles. Sheep were being sent from Scotland or Wales across the Channel to France and even to Italy.

And worse threats were on the horizon. Live exports, particularly of sheep, were poised to escalate with alarming rapidity. And a new EC Directive was fatally to weaken the UK's legal protections for animals being transported.

There was, however, a major silver lining: the continuing and growing volume of public concern and protest.

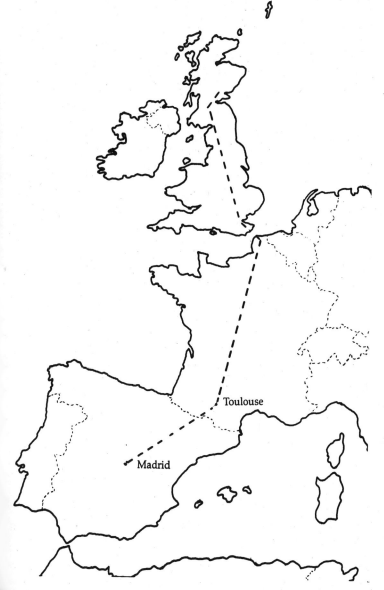

October 1989: Lambs sent from Scotland to Toulouse (30hrs). In breach of the export licence some lambs continued on to a Madrid slaughterhouse

Part Two

The Live Trade Today

Chapter Eight

Spanish Slaughterhouses and French Farmers

Lobby of Parliament

With the start of the new decade, Compassion in World Farming decided that the time had come to increase the pressure for a ban on live exports. On 28th June 1990, we organised a mass lobby of Parliament. Over 800 CIWF supporters joined the lobby, which had the support of 26 other animal welfare societies.

The day began with a Press Conference. Ron Davies MP, Labour's front bench agricultural spokesman, called the huge rise of calf exports to the Netherlands 'not tolerable' and he promised that Labour will 'accept the case for a policy of slaughtering as near as possible to the point of production'. Also speaking vigorously against the live trade were Carla Lane, David Shepherd, Peter O'Sullevan, the Liberal Democrat spokesman Matthew Taylor MP and Sir Richard Body MP, the Conservative backbencher who in 1991 was, through his Private Member's Bill, to secure the banning in the UK of sow stalls and tethers.

During the lobby a lively debate was in progress in the House of Commons. Mr Gummer, the Minister of Agriculture, acknowledged the presence of 'today's lobby ... led by Compassion in World Farming'. Tony Banks pointed out: 'I appreciate that the Secretary of State is a voracious carnivore and likely to eat anything with legs other than a table; but is he aware that, despite his assurances to the House, a great deal of suffering is still caused to animals moved out of Britain for slaughter'.

The lobby itself was a huge success with many people meeting their MPs and having the opportunity to tell them of their welfare concerns.

Article 36

At the Press Conference, Peter Roberts said that if the European Community was not willing to end the live trade, the UK government should go it alone and ban live exports, acting in reliance on Article 36 of the Treaty of Rome.

A great deal was to be heard of Article 36 during the 90's. Article 34 of the Treaty of Rome (which is the cornerstone of EC law) prohibits EC Member States from imposing restrictions on exports. (Article 30 similarly prohibits restrictions on imports.)

Article 36, however, enables a Member State to impose restrictions on imports or exports where these can be justified on grounds of public morality or public policy or on grounds of the protection of health and life of humans or animals.

Peter Roberts' argument was that Article 36 would allow the UK government to ban live exports as the trade is clearly offensive to UK 'public morality'.

The government, however, takes a very cautious view of Article 36 and interprets it much more narrowly than a common sense reading would suggest. They stress that in previous cases the European Court of Justice has decided that a Member State can no longer rely on Article 36 in a particular field of the law once the EC has made Directives or Regulations covering that field.

Thus it is argued that because the EC has issued a Directive on the transport of animals, an individual Member State cannot rely on the public morality clause of Article 36 to ban live exports.

Whilst certain court cases indeed support this interpretation, it is nonetheless an extremely unadventurous approach to the possibilities of Article 36. We will return to this subject when looking at the export of animals to Spanish abattoirs,

Compassion in World Farming's court case against John Gummer and the export of calves.

Slaughter in Spain

The UK government had for many years refused to allow animals to be sent to Spain for slaughter. This was because Spain had not implemented the EC Directive (74/577/EEC) requiring animals to be stunned before slaughter.

In 1990 however, the government was coming under increasing pressure from the European Commission in Brussels to grant licences allowing animals to be sent to Spain for slaughter.

Compassion in World Farming sent an investigator to Spain in order to find out what was really happening in Spanish abattoirs. During his visit he made a video which showed scenes of horrendous cruelty.

The video shows sheep and lambs being slaughtered at the Matadero de Valdetorres de Jarama slaughterhouse near Madrid on 17th October 1990. None of the animals were stunned (rendered unconscious) before slaughter. The lambs were shackled by one hind leg and, hanging upside down, they struggled – often for two minutes or more – until the slaughterman was ready to slit their throats. Even the slaughter cut was not always performed adequately and many lambs could be seen still struggling and obviously conscious several minutes later as they slowly bled to death.

The video then shows cattle being slaughtered at the Afrivaso Val Mojado slaughterhouse at Toledo on 18th October 1990. Although a captive bolt pistol was being used for stunning, the pistol was not being applied in the correct position at the centre of the forehead. Cows can be seen obviously still conscious, staggering and falling down, only to be shackled by the hind leg and slaughtered.

Shortly afterwards the RSPCA also filmed horrendous scenes in other Spanish abattoirs. Formal complaints were made to the Commission in Brussels. Spain, however, managed to persuade the Commission that it had put its slaughterhouses in order. Pressure then began to mount once more for Britain to export animals for slaughter to Spain.

Compassion in World Farming had its doubts and decided to return to Spain, visiting the Centelles slaughterhouse near Barcelona on 19th June 1991. A new film showed sheep being shackled upside down and having their throats cut without any attempt whatsoever at pre-stunning. After two minutes they were placed on wooden cradles – the film shows one sheep pathetically trying to lift its blood-soaked head at this moment.

A formal complaint was made to the Spanish Agriculture Minister and to the EC Agriculture Commissioner, Ray MacSharry.

It is worth noting that the UK's action in banning animals being sent to Spain for slaughter was arguably in breach of the Treaty of Rome's provision barring restrictions on exports. If challenged, the UK government would have had to rely on Article 36 of the Treaty which allows a Member State to impose restrictions on exports where this can be justified on the ground of 'public morality'. It is ironic that the government which so often claimed that Article 36 was virtually a dead letter, was in fact relying on it in refusing to send animals to Spain.

The attitude of the Commission was that even though Spain was in breach of EC law in not pre-stunning animals, the UK was not entitled to refuse to export animals to Spain for slaughter.

Sadly, there is no happy ending to this tale. On 1st January 1993 there came into force a new EC Transport Directive (91/628/EEC) which insisted with increased vigour that Member States must allow animals to be transported throughout the Community. The UK government caved in and announced that from January 1993 British lambs and other farm animals could be exported to Spanish slaughterhouses. It is a pity that the government did not stand firm and risk being taken to the European Court, which could have considered the applicability of Article 36 in these circumstances. Surely 'public morality' (the Article 36 words) requires that animals should not be sent to Spain to be slaughtered in defiance of EC law and common humanity.

CIWF takes Minister to High Court

The summer and autumn of 1990 saw a number of brutal attacks on imported sheep by French farmers, who believed that such imports were threatening their livelihood.

On 28th July, 94 British sheep were poisoned to death with phosdrin, a powerful insecticide, at a farm at St. Laurent sur Sevre.[1]

Then on 23rd August a lorry carrying 439 British sheep was hi-jacked in Thouars, Brittany, and set alight. The driver managed to release about half the sheep (which were in such a bad way they had to be slaughtered anyway), but 219 were burned to death in the lorry.[2] A police official reported that 'the sheep screamed in agony as they were burned alive'.[3]

Shortly afterwards, on 29th August, farmers in Normandy intercepted two trucks carrying Irish sheep and British calves and turned them loose in the streets of Saint Lo.[4] 300 Dutch sheep were released from a lorry at Limoges and set to graze on a lawn treated with a fertiliser designed to make their flesh unfit for human consumption for a month.[5]

A further outrage followed on 6th September when 200 French farmers ambushed a lorry carrying 386 British sheep outside Bellac, near Limoges. The Times reported that the driver was stopped by a barricade of burning tyres. He was forced to take the lambs to the Mayor's garden and then on to the local abattoir where they were slaughtered.[6] Their carcases were then set on fire and, according to the Daily Telegraph, strewn in the government offices.[7] French police looked on, but did nothing.

The Times and Daily Telegraph also reported another incident in which farmers hi-jacked a lorry at Nyons and turned the sheep on to the streets. They later killed and burned some of the animals.

Throughout this period the French police and authorities appeared unable or unwilling to act. M. Lacombe, the French farmers' union leader, said that he was powerless to stop the violent actions of his members.[8]

The pattern of violence was repeated on 26th September when a lorry load of 545 British sheep was hi-jacked near Bourges in central France. The lorry was forced to stop by a car which cut in front of it, blocking its path. Some 60 farmers with staves and metal bars were lying in wait. Some were throwing around a sheep's head which was still dripping with blood (this appeared not to come from the sheep in the lorry as it was cold; this would suggest that the head came from an animal killed some time earlier). The crowd battered the lorry and tried to drag sheep by their heads through the truck's ventilation slats. Eventually the truck was taken to the abattoir.[9]

The Agriculture Minister, Mr John Gummer, had earlier protested to the French authorities, but they seemed quite unable to quell what had become known as the 'lamb wars'.

A farmer at Limoges was reported as having said that he and about 35 others had organised weapon caches and plans for a sustained campaign against deliveries of foreign meat to French slaughterhouses.[10] The European newspaper reported that French farmers had demonstrated in Nevers. Six policemen were hurt in clashes with a group of marchers who tried to tear down the prefecture's gates. Most participants left the city peacefully but more than 800 farmers armed with sticks and stones clashed with riot squads.[11]

The Independent reported that the French Ministry of the Interior had drafted in 2,000 extra police including 14 riot squad divisions. The report added that the Agriculture Ministry seemed privately to despair of bringing the most militant elements under control.[12]

The British Agriculture Ministry resolutely refused to ban live exports to France. One of their arguments was that a ban would be seen as the British giving in to French terrorism. Games of machismo were being played out with live animals as the weapons.

Compassion in World Farming decided that the only way forward was to bring court proceedings against the Minister of Agriculture. They filed papers seeking judicial review of the

Minister's decision to continue granting licences for the export of sheep to France at a time when they were at risk of being poisoned, burned or otherwise attacked by French farmers.[13] Judicial review is a procedure in which the court is asked to declare that someone acting in an official capacity has acted unlawfully, i.e. outwith his legal powers. The RSPCA later brought similar proceedings.

The case centred around the Export of Animals (Protection) Order 1981. Article 3(2) provided that the Minister 'shall not grant a [export] licence unless he is satisfied that the arrangements for transporting the animals to their final destination are such as to protect them from unnecessary suffering'.

Compassion in World Farming argued that after the first burnings and poisonings it was clear that further animals were at risk of being killed or injured and that therefore the Minister could not possibly have been satisfied (as he was required by law to be) that the arrangements were such as to protect the animals from unnecessary suffering. The argument was that he had acted contrary to Article 3(2) in continuing to grant export licences.

The Minister argued that he could not refuse to grant licences as to do so would be contrary to Article 34 of the Treaty of Rome which prohibits restrictions on exports.

Compassion in World Farming disagreed. They pointed to Article 36 of the Treaty which allows a Member State to impose restrictions on exports where this can be justified on grounds of public morality or the protection of health and life of animals. Compassion in World Farming argued that Article 36 enabled the Minister to refuse to grant licences for the export of sheep to France during the 'lamb wars'.

Readers will remember that some European legal cases suggest that once an EC Directive has been enacted laying down detailed provisions in a particular field, Article 36 may no longer be relied upon in that field. It is known as an 'occupied field', i.e. occupied by the relevant Directive. The thinking appears to be that once a Directive has laid down rules on a certain human or animal health issue, it is no longer open for a Member State to go further in seeking to protect human or animal health in its own territory.

In the 'lamb wars' case the Judge had to decide whether the Minister had been justified in taking the view that he could not have relied on Article 36 had he wished to ban sheep exports to France.

The Judge ruled that the Minister was justified in believing that he could not rely on Article 36. Significantly the Judge did not give as a ground for his ruling the fact that there were two EC Directives in force in this field. The Judge took the view that, on the facts of the case, the Minister was justified in believing that it would not have been 'proportionate' for him to impose a total ban on the export of sheep to France. (One principle of European law is that action taken under Article 36 must be proportionate to the problem you are attempting to solve.)

The salient aspect from the viewpoint of Article 36, is that the Court did not declare (nor did the Minister seek to argue) that the Minister was prevented from relying on Article 36 by the mere fact that a Transport Directive was in existence.

Although the court case was lost it proved hugely successful in highlighting the misery of live exports and in demonstrating to the government that, when they had a strong legal case, Compassion in World Farming was willing to take court action to safeguard welfare.

In 1991 the French attacks were renewed. A lorry containing 400 British lambs was halted by a barricade. The lambs had to be rescued by police.

In late October three loads of British lambs were released into the streets of Bourges. The 1200 lambs were rounded up and counted back on to the lorries, but 100 were missing and some were dead.[14]

Stern magazine

An appalling tale of the brutality and neglect involved in the transport of live animals in Europe was told in the May 1991 edition of *Stern*, a German magazine.

Hundreds of thousands of horses are imported into the EC from Eastern Europe. They mainly go to Italy, France and Belgium.

The journey from Poland to the Italian border may take almost 3 days, some of the way being on tracks full of pot-holes.

One Polish lorry portrayed by *Stern* was so low that the horses were forced to travel for days with their heads bent. Agonised by this unnatural stance and by thirst, the animals lash out and wound each other.

And it's not just horses. A lorry carrying 150 sheep breaks down near Hanover. The driver leaves it to be towed away, going to a hotel to get some sleep. Eventually a passer-by alerts the police. The sheep had been squashed in together to an unbelievable degree, and the ventilation was quite inadequate. By the time they were found, 73 sheep had died of suffocation.

On a hot day at Mannheim Station, freight wagons containing bulls arrive after a 24 hour journey. They are shunted into a siding where they stand for hours in the searing heat. Alerted by blood dripping on the track, workers eventually open the wagon and are met by a gruesome sight. Confined in the wagon in temperatures of 100 degrees and more, and with inadequate ventilation, the bulls had panicked and had attacked and wounded each other. 'One, wedged in by the corpses of others, had no longer enough room to fall, and had perished standing up.'

Chapter Nine

New EC Directive: 1991

From the beginning of the 90's there was much talk of '1992'. This referred to the fact that 1992 (in fact 1st January 1993) had been selected as the date on which the Single European Market was to come into operation. This meant that all barriers to trade had to be stripped away – and that included the trade in live animals.

Accordingly, the Commission published a proposed new Directive. This eventually came into force on 1st January 1993 and is entitled 'EC Directive on the Protection of Animals during Transport'. Despite its title, the Directive's primary purpose is to ensure the free movement of live animals throughout the Community. Welfare needs come a very poor second and are not allowed to impede the free trade goal.

Before the Directive became law, long battles were fought. From the outset it was clear that it would be highly detrimental to animal welfare as it was designed to lead to a big increase in the number of animals being trucked around Europe.

For many years Compassion in World Farming and other bodies had campaigned for the live trade to be brought to an end. Compassion in World Farming believes that, as long as the meat trade persists, animals should be sent to a slaughterhouse as near as possible to the farm, with the fresh meat being transported throughout the EC. The principle of slaughter as near as possible to the farm is often translated into a call for an overall 8-hour journey limit to be imposed throughout the EC.

The Commission's proposed Directive made no concession

to such thinking. Instead it simply repeated the provision in the existing 1977 Directive which only required animals to be given food and water every 24 hours.

It is worth clarifying that a journey limit is a quite different thing from feeding and watering intervals. The latter are times after which animals must be given food and water. Once that has been done and they have had any stipulated rest, the journey can start up again. A journey limit, on the other hand, is an overall limit, after which the animals must have reached their final destination.

The European Parliament appointed David Morris MEP as rapporteur for the proposed Directive. (When the European Parliament considers a proposal, it first appoints one of its members to prepare a report to aid the Parliament's debate).

The Morris Report was critical of the Commission's proposal. The Parliament, recognising the paucity of the Commission's proposal, voted for a maximum 8-hour journey time for animals being transported for slaughter.

The Commission does not have to accept the Parliament's amendments. In this case, however, they accepted the Parliament's principle that there should be a maximum journey limit while rejecting the specific of an 8-hour limit. The Commission added a recital (the recitals set out the thinking behind a Directive) to their proposal stating:

> whereas it is unnecessary for live animals for slaughter to be transported over long distances as modern technology permits the rapid transport of carcases, either chilled or frozen, to all parts of the Community.

Meanwhile in the UK, the House of Commons Agriculture Committee had been considering the welfare implications of the proposed Directive. Their Report on Animals in Transit was published on 20th June 1991. The Committee stated that they believed that the transport of animals for slaughter over long distances was undesirable, adding that:

> The Commission should frame legislation which

expressly discourages the transportation of slaughter animals over long distances.

All this thinking – of the European Parliament, of the Commission, of the Commons Agriculture Committee – was totally ignored by the EC Council of•Agriculture Ministers. The new Directive (91/628/EEC), agreed by the Council on 21st October 1991, placed no limit whatsoever on slaughter journeys.

The deliberations of the Council are generally conducted in private. It is, however, understood that only the German Minister pressed for an overall journey limit. The British government likes to portray itself as one of the EC's leaders when it comes to animal welfare, but they apparently failed to support the Germans. Indeed, in May 1993, Earl Howe, speaking in the House of Lords on behalf of the Ministry of Agriculture, made it clear that the government does not support an 8-hour journey limit – he condemned this as 'unduly restrictive'.

Within the doom generated by the Directive there was one piece of good news for the British public. For a long time it had looked as if the Directive would force the UK to lift its ban on horses being sent abroad for slaughter.

The public had been outraged by this possibility and the British Horse Society and the International League for the Protection of Horses led a long campaign against this threat. At first the EC was adamant in insisting that the UK must allow horses to be exported, arguing that the fundamental principles of the Directive and of the Treaty of Rome would be breached, if one country were allowed to keep an export ban.

Eventually, however, the British campaign wore them down. The 1991 Directive contains in its small print a clause which in effect allows the UK to retain the Minimum Values Order. It is this Order – which prohibits the export for slaughter of horses worth less than a certain value – which effectively stops horses being sent overseas for slaughter.

We may not have heard the last of this battle. What the Directive says is that the Commission must at some future unspecified time propose detailed rules protecting horses in transit and that, until such rules are adopted, individual Member States may retain their national rules. If one day such EC-wide rules are made, the UK will be told – 'Look, we have made rules which will protect horses wherever they are transported within the EC, now the British must come into line and allow horses to be exported for slaughter'.

Weakening of UK law

The bad news was that the Directive forced the UK to downgrade some of its legal protections for animals in transit.

Some Directives only set minimum standards; they allow an individual Member State to have stricter laws if it wants to. The 1991 Transport Directive is different. Each Member State's law must follow the Directive; it cannot be weaker, nor can it be tougher. The reason for this is that the EC believes that if one Member State has tougher rules than another, that distorts trade, and that is a cardinal sin in the EC's book.

And so UK law had to be downgraded in three areas as from 1st January 1993 when the Directive came into force.

Firstly, animals may now travel for up to 15 hours in the UK without being given food and water (formerly the maximum time was 12 hours except where the journey could be completed within 15 hours).

Secondly, as we have seen, the government dropped its ban on animals being sent to Spain for slaughter.

Finally, there is the question of the port lairages. Until the end of 1992, before crossing the Channel, animals had, by law, to be rested for 10 hours at a lairage near one of the ports. There they had to be given food and water and inspected by a vet to ensure that they were still fit to travel. This meant that animals at least started their journey into Europe in a refreshed state. These breaks were vital because by the time they got to the Channel, some of the animals had travelled from as far afield as Scotland and North Wales.

These compulsory port breaks were swept away by the 1991 Directive which condemned them as a barrier to trade. In 1992, 28,072 animals were declared unfit to travel when inspected by vets at the port lairages. Now there is nothing to stop these unfit animals being forced to continue their journeys into Europe.

There has been much talk of how being part of the EC leads to a loss of national sovereignty for the UK. The field of animal transport provides a clear example of what this means in practice – the UK can no longer retain the laws it wishes to have to protect animals in transit.

Take a raincheck on the details

In many ways the 1991 Directive represented the worst of all possible worlds. It was precisely the opposite of having your cake and eating it in that it insisted on animals being trucked around Europe but contained very few of the detailed rules needed to safeguard their welfare. All the really important things were to follow on at a later date.

Under Article 13 of the Directive the Commission was, by 1st July 1992, to publish detailed proposals on:
– maximum journey times
– feeding and watering intervals and rest periods
– vehicle standards and maximum stocking densities.

The Directive stipulated that the Commission was to base its proposals on a report by the Scientific Veterinary Committee (SVC). The Committee's report was published on 30th April 1992.[1] Despite this, the Commission's proposals were not produced until July 1993, over a year after the due date. We will return to these proposals and the SVC report at a later stage.

Enforcement

No laws will be effective unless transporters know that breaches of the law are likely to be discovered and that, in serious cases, prosecution is likely to follow. This question was considered by the Report of the Commons Agriculture Committee, which was referred to earlier.

The Report quotes the British Veterinary Association as saying: 'We do not believe that our present regulations are enforced at all'. They added that in their experience 'very rarely will a vehicle have been stopped'. This view was echoed by the Road Haulage Association which told the Committee: 'The risk of being apprehended whilst operating illegally is small, and to many it is a risk worth taking'.

The Ministry of Agriculture on the contrary, said that there were over 200,000 vehicle checks in the year ending 31st March 1990. Only 5%, however, of the infringements revealed by such checks were prosecuted. Compassion in World Farming believes that there must be a high level of both inspections and prosecutions if welfare regulations are to be consistently observed. This view was shared by the Committee:

> We therefore want these checks to be more stringent, so that hauliers and drivers become well aware that non-compliance with the law will be detected and penalised.

Sadly, most EC countries and the Commission give a very low priority to enforcement of the welfare in transit rules. Indeed, in an explanatory memorandum to its 1993 proposals, the Commission conceded that the rules on feeding and watering are 'systematically flouted'.[2]

The Commission's veterinary inspectorate is underfunded and understaffed. Moreover, the inspectorate's time is spent on monitoring compliance with veterinary regulations, not on welfare. The inspectorate must be given sufficient resources to do its job properly.

One serious defect is that the Commission cannot itself enforce European laws in the individual Member States. That would be to interfere with their sovereignty. Enforcement, says the Commission, is the responsibility of the Member States. All the Commission can do is inspect whether the Member States themselves are properly enforcing the law. The Commission's inspectors inspect the Member States' inspectors to see if they are enforcing the law, which in most cases they are not. And so we have a grave and courteous dance, in which no one steps on anyone's toes and no effective policing is achieved.

Chapter Ten

Export of Calves

The veal crate

Most animals sent abroad are intended for slaughter on, or soon after, arrival at their destination. This is not, however, the fate of young calves, most of whom are destined for the veal crate, a system so cruel that its use has been banned in the UK since 1st January 1990.[1]

After sheep and lambs, calves are nowadays the second largest group of animals exported from the UK. In the early 1980's live cattle exports consisted of both calves and older animals, mainly cull cows, being sent abroad for slaughter. By the early 1990's, however, the picture had changed with the majority of live cattle exports being calves.[2] In 1990, the UK exported 338,806 calves. This figure rose to 399,599 in 1991 and to 420,620 in 1992. Trade sources warn that at least 450,000 – possibly even half a million – could be shipped overseas by 1994.[3]

The majority are sent to Holland or France, where most will be reared in veal crate farms.

Most of the calves used in the veal trade are the bull calves of dairy cows. They obviously cannot be used as dairy cow replacements, nor are they the right breed for rearing on for beef. The infant calf is removed from its mother at a day or two old – a process which appears to involve extreme distress for both. The calf is then sent to market when it is about one week old. From there it may well be sent to a veal crate farm in Europe.

As mentioned earlier, the veal crate is a solid-sided wooden box which is so narrow that, from the age of about two weeks, the calves cannot even turn round. As they get older the calves cannot even lie down in a normal, stretched-out position.

The calf remains in the crate for the rest of its life – which can be anything up to 26 weeks. Throughout that time it stands or lies on the slatted wooden floor. It is given no straw or other bedding material. Why? Because if it ate the straw, its flesh might deepen in colour to a healthy red. But European consumers want their veal to be of the palest pink tone – so much so that it is referred to as 'white veal'.

To achieve this, the calf is denied the roughage and fibre which it craves, being fed throughout its life on an all-liquid diet, of milk powder mixed with water. The iron content is kept deliberately low in a further attempt to keep the flesh pale. Many of the calves are verging on clinical anaemia by the time they are slaughtered. Professor John Webster, the UK's leading cattle expert, declares that this type of diet 'completely distorts the normal development of the rumen', the calf's stomach system.[4] In a desperate attempt to get solid food, the calves lick at their wooden boxes and swallow their own hair.

The crate also prevents calves having any social contact with their fellows. Anyone who has seen young calves out in a field will know how they love to play together. In the crate the only time they even glimpse another calf is at feeding time – once or twice a day when the fronts of their crates are opened to allow them to drink their liquid diet from a bucket.

As we have seen, the use of the veal crate has been illegal in the UK since 1990.

In 1984, Peter Roberts, Director of Compassion in World Farming, brought criminal proceedings against a farm which operated the crate system. The essence of the argument was that the system was inherently cruel. Offences were alleged under the Protection of Animals Act 1911 and under Section 1 of the Agriculture (Miscellaneous Provisions) Act 1968 which makes it an offence to cause unnecessary pain or unnecessary distress to any livestock.

The Ministry of Agriculture had on a number of occasions said that it relied on the very real value of its Welfare Codes.

Compassion in World Farming was able to show that the Codes were difficult to enforce, ineffective in action and were widely considered in farming circles to be a sop to public opinion, designed to reduce the pressure being put on the government by the electorate.

The case was lost, but not in vain. The public concern generated by the case led eventually to the banning of the crate by The Welfare of Calves Regulations 1987, which came into force on 1st January 1990. These require calves to be able to turn round without difficulty in their pens and to have sufficient iron for full health and vigour.

Has the ban led to an increase in exports?

Some people have tried to argue that the ban on the veal crate in the UK has led to an increase in the number of calves being exported for rearing in overseas veal crate farms.

This argument is simply not supported by the facts. Even before the ban there were relatively few veal crate farms in the UK. As a result, the ban affected only a small number of farmers and cannot account for the huge number of calves being exported each year. The truth of the matter is that long before the UK ban, large numbers of calves were shipped annually to European veal crates.

It should, moreover, be stressed that the UK ban does not compel farmers to export their calves. Calves can quite legally be reared for veal in the UK as long as some form of group housing system is used.

The export of calves

Each day the UK exports over 1,100 calves, most of which will end up in the very system we have outlawed here. Compassion in World Farming believes that it is morally unacceptable for the UK, having recognised the cruelty of the veal crate by prohibiting its use, to continue to send calves overseas for rearing in crates. The proper way forward is for the UK government to ensure the veal crate ban is adopted throughout the EC. In the meantime, Compassion in World

Farming believes that the export of calves should be banned where the animals are to be reared in veal crates.

The Ministry of Agriculture has refused to do so, arguing that a ban would be in breach of the Treaty of Rome, the legal cornerstone of the European Community. In particular, the Ministry contends that Article 34 of the Treaty, which prohibits restrictions on exports to other Member States, prevents a ban on the export of calves.

In response, Compassion in World Farming has drawn attention to Article 36 which, as we have seen, enables a Member State to impose prohibitions or restrictions on imports or exports where these can be justified on grounds of 'public morality, public policy . . . the protection of health and life of humans, animals . . .'.

It is clear from a 1980 case that if the public policy and public morality parts of Article 36 are to be relied on to ban imports or exports, the activity in question must be unlawful within the State wishing to impose the import or export ban.[5] In other words, a Member State cannot say that a particular trade is so offensive that it wishes to ban imports or exports of the goods in question, if it has not found that activity sufficiently offensive to ban it within its own territory. If the British government were to ban the export of calves for rearing in veal crates, it would be able successfully to mount this legal hurdle as the use of the crate is unlawful in the UK.

As we have seen, there are some European legal cases which suggest that once an EC Directive has been enacted laying down detailed rules in a particular field, Article 36 may no longer be relied on in that field. (This is called the 'occupied fields' principle).

There is indeed a 1991 EC Directive laying down minimum standards for the rearing of calves although, appallingly, it fails to prohibit veal crates.[6]

Compassion in World Farming nonetheless believes that there are a number of legal arguments the UK government could use to show why a ban on the export of calves would be different from the earlier cases which prevent Article 36 being used when an EC Directive is in place in the field in question. Some of these arguments can be summed up as follows:

1 *Distinction between imports and exports*

The final sentence of Article 36 stresses that the Article cannot be used to justify what is in reality 'a means of arbitrary discrimination or a disguised restriction on trade between Member States'.

When a Member State imposes *import* restrictions and seeks to rely on Article 36, the suspicion can easily arise that the State is really trying to protect its own producers. In the case of an *export* restriction, the UK is much less likely to be accused of trying to gain an advantage for UK producers. No conceivable benefit could accrue to UK farmers if the export of calves to veal crate farms was prohibited.

2 *Public morality/public policy*

Previous cases leading to the 'occupied fields' principle have in general been concerned with the human and animal health part of Article 36 and not with its reference to public morality and public policy.

The question of whether a particular rearing system is so cruel that its use should be restricted is one not just of animal health, but of public morality and public policy. Public concern in this country was such that in 1990 the UK banned the use of the veal crate. Public morality in the UK has determined that the veal crate is unacceptable and it is perfectly reasonable for that public morality to go on to say: and we do not wish calves to be exported to other parts of the EC for rearing in the very system that we have outlawed in the UK.

3 *Developing body of law*

Following on from the previous section, it should be emphasised that European law is a young and developing body of law which is by no means rigidly set. For Ministry lawyers to assert that no reliance can be placed on Article 36 is to ignore the developing nature of European law. New cases are regularly giving fresh clarification on that law's interpretation.

One example of this is Anita Groener v. the Minister for Education, and City of Dublin Vocational Education Committee [1990] 1. C.M.L.R. 401.[7] This case concerned the free movement of EC workers and the prohibition on discrimination against Community nationals. The Irish authorities had refused a teaching post in commercial art to a Dutch woman because she failed a test of knowledge of the Irish language; it should be noted that the course was to be taught in English.

To the surprise of many lawyers, the European Court held that the approach of the Irish authorities was lawful and that the national policy of promoting the Irish language was legitimate in terms of Community law and could even override the free movement of EC workers provided that the restriction (i.e. the requirement to pass an Irish language test) was necessary to attain the aim of the policy and was not otherwise discriminating or disproportionate.

Following on from this case it could be argued that it is necessary, in order to fulfil the British policy that calves should not be reared in crates, to prohibit calves being sent to veal crate farms in other parts of the EC.

4 *Greater power for individual Member States*

There has in the 90's been much debate about what properly falls within the province of the European Community and what should instead be decided by the individual Member States.

Many feel that much more ought to be left to the Member States. In this context, Article 36 is vital in providing that the morality or policy of an individual country can take precedence over free trade. It may well be that, in the new climate emphasising the need for individual countries not to be swamped by the EC, Article 36 will be given great importance by the Courts.

In conclusion, Compassion in World Farming believes that if

the UK government were to be taken to the European Court of Justice for banning the export of calves, it would have some good legal arguments with which to defend itself.

From the point of view of both morality and common sense, the export of calves to veal crates should be banned. It is absurd to judge a system to be sufficiently cruel for its use to be banned in the UK and to then go on to say: 'Oh yes, but it is OK to send our calves abroad to be reared in this system'.

In 1991, Labour MP Chris Mullin tabled a Bill, drafted for him by Compassion in World Farming, designed to end the export of calves to veal crate units.

Mr Mullin made a moving speech to the House of Commons describing the cruelties of the crate – the all-liquid diet, the inability to turn round, the slippery, slatted floors, the lack of companionship. Sadly, the government refused to let the Bill become law.

Stresses of transport

So far this chapter has been concerned with the fact that the majority of exported calves end up in veal crates. However, the journey from the UK to the Continent is itself also a major problem. After being bought at a bustling and confusing cattle market, the calves – often only one week old – endure the further stress of the journey to the exporting port, such as Harwich or Dover, and the sea journey to the European mainland with yet more road transport on arrival.

One scientific study by Trunkfield and Broom of Cambridge University's Department of Clinical Veterinary Medicine concludes that 'transport normally leads to poor welfare in calves'.[8]

They add that research shows that handling by people and transport 'can be a severe stress for animals'. They then examine the aspects of transport which lead to stress for calves.

Loading and unloading are considered by some researchers to be the most stressful stages of transport. This is due to the physical exertion involved, the noise and the contact with people who handle the animals during loading and unloading.

Modern rearing methods mean that animals do not become familiar with people. Trunkfield and Broom write that, as a result, 'the slightest contact with humans can initiate a substantial fear response'.

Stress also arises from the fact that transport inevitably means putting the calf in an environment (the inside of the truck) which he will never have experienced before. Moreover, transport frequently involves mixing animals from different herds. This mixing of unfamiliar animals in a confined space is a major stress factor and can lead to aggression.

Trunkfield and Broom go on to identify the following as additional stressful elements: fluctuating temperatures, deprivation of food and water and, sometimes in the case of very young calves, weaning. They conclude:

> The disturbance for the animal is psychological as well as physical and physiological. Calf welfare during transit may be very poor.

The problems are highlighted by the fact that mortality rates are higher for calves which undergo transportation than for those which do not.[9] A 1974 study showed that 60% of 1,769 calves younger than two weeks which were transported, fell ill during the following four weeks, and 21% died.[10] Another study showed that calves, particularly those who are very young and travel over long distances, often die following transportation.[11]

Bearing in mind the considerable stress imposed on calves by transport, Compassion in World Farming believes that (subject to limited exceptions) the transport of these young animals should be brought to an end.

Chapter Eleven

The Road to Misery: 1992–1993

Massive increase in live exports

Ministry of Agriculture figures show that 773,000 lambs and sheep were exported in 1991 as compared with 488,000 in 1990. In 1992, 1,373,000 were exported, an increase of over half a million on 1991. At the time of writing no official figures are available for 1993. It is, however, estimated by trade sources that some 2,000,000 sheep and lambs were exported in 1993.

Almost 400,000 calves were exported in 1991, an increase of 60,000 on 1990. In 1992 the figure rose to 420,000. The estimate for 1993 is 450,000.

Table: Export figures for the 90's

	1990	1991	1992	1993
Lambs and sheep	488,908	773,502	1,373,657	2,000,000*
Calves	338,806	399,599	420,620	450,000*

* Estimates

Source: Ministry of Agriculture, Fisheries and Food

The Road to Misery

In the summer of 1992 Compassion in World Farming released a new video, *The Road to Misery*, which highlighted the horrifying reality of transport in the Europe of the 90's. Extracts were shown by the BBC, ITV and many European television stations; it even reached Japan.

The film shows sheep being subjected to religious slaughter

in a Paris abattoir, battered Polish horses en route to French slaughterhouses and sheep being slaughtered without pre-stunning in Spain.

The image which most haunted people was of a bull with a broken hip on a ship in Croatia being repeatedly prodded in the genitals with an electric goad in an effort to get him to stand up. When this fails, his front leg is shackled and he is hoisted out of the ship and dumped on the quay. Later there is a change of mind. It is decided that it would be financially advantageous to 'lose' the bull at sea. So he is hauled on to a fork lift and shoved back on board, banging his head on the ship's metal railings as he falls.

After the film was shown on television, Compassion in World Farming asked viewers to send postcards expressing their horror to the Ministry of Agriculture. As a result, the Ministry was flooded with 25,000 postcards from the public calling for a ban on live exports.

The law routinely ignored

As we have seen, EC law only requires animals to be given food and water every 24 hours. Recent scientific evidence shows that for most animals this is quite insufficient.[1]

However, even this unsatisfactory provision is hardly ever observed. Indeed, as we have seen, in July 1993 the Commission conceded that the law on feeding and watering is 'systematically flouted'.[2] This is a major step forward. Previously the authorities in both the UK and the EC have tended to dismiss evidence of breaches of the law as 'isolated incidents'.

Some of the evidence which brought the Commission to this conclusion emerged in 1991 and 1992 when the Dutch Animal Welfare Society and the RSPCA trailed ten journeys, most of which involved pigs going from Holland to Italy. In *all* ten journeys no attempt was made to give food or water to the animals, even though nine of the journeys were over 30 hours. In the worst case, pigs went 59 hours without food and water.[3]

Each year some three million pigs are exported from

—|—|—|—|—|—|—|—   Sheep going from Scotland to Southern Italy (over 40 hrs)

—•—•—•—•—•—•—   Pigs going from Holland to Southern Italy (over 35 hrs)

Holland to other EC countries. British exports of fattening pigs leapt in 1991 to 236,000.

The sad fact is that pigs make rotten travellers, sometimes beginning to suffer from dehydration after just 6 hours. They are likely to get motion sickness during road transport.[4] To avoid pigs vomiting and dying on the journey, they are usually fasted for 16–24 hours before departure. This may be the lesser of two evils – but it remains an unjustifiable cruelty. Pigs simply should not be involved in long journeys.

Two of the trails referred to earlier followed consignments of sheep from Britain to Southern Italy. Appallingly the sheep were given neither food nor water during the journeys, which lasted 44 and 47 hours.

One of these trails was reported on BBC Radio 4's *Face the Facts*. What was particularly galling was that it would have been perfectly easy for the driver to care for the sheep. At the Italian border he stopped at a lairage – a place designed for animals to be given food and water. Here the driver ate a meal and rested himself, but ignored the sheep.

Petitions

In 1992 the veterinary profession added its weight to the protests against the cruelties of the live trade. Professor Ronald Anderson and Dr Jane Hunter of Liverpool University's Veterinary School organised a petition calling for a maximum journey time of 8 hours and for animals to be slaughtered as near as possible to the farm of rearing. The petition was supported by the British Veterinary Association and the BVA Animal Welfare Foundation.

On 23rd July 1992, the petition bearing 3,000 veterinary signatures was presented to Mr Gummer, the Agriculture Minister. The support of the veterinary profession gives an enormous boost to the campaign to end the long distance transport of animals.

Within Europe, Eurogroup for Animal Welfare collected a massive 2,111,962 signatures on a petition calling on the Community to introduce an 8-hour limit on the journeys of live animals to slaughter. What is shocking is the continued refusal of the Council of Ministers to recognise the widespread revulsion felt by so many members of the public.

New German film

At the end of June 1993 a shocking new film was shown on German television. It follows cattle being sent from Germany to southern Europe and then on by sea to the Middle East.

In the worst incident, in Romania, a crane is used to off-load cattle which are too weak to stand. A chain is tied round the animal's horns. Then it is lifted by the crane out of the truck and set down on the quay. While one animal is in the air, the skin of its head tears, the horn breaks and it falls to the ground from a height of two metres. Its back legs are paralysed. The animal writhes in pain on the ground. It is left all day and all night on the quay – in the icy cold.

In France we see animals who have been starved of water for over 30 hours. Once on board ship they may remain another 30 hours without water. Some break down; others are demented by thirst. Sometimes over 40 cattle die on the sea voyage to Egypt.

Amazingly, this appalling trade is subsidised by the EC taxpayer. Generous subsidies are paid to dealers who export cattle to countries outside the EC. They are being rewarded for not adding to the EC beef mountain. These subsidies are in addition to whatever sums the exporter receives from the purchaser of the animals. In a letter the European Commission admitted:

> Export restitutions are paid in order to encourage the export of animals which would otherwise be slaughtered in the Community and whose meat could then add to our already large stocks.

Oblivious to the outcry generated by the use of taxpayers' money to subsidise this trade the Commission added:

> This system [of export subsidies] has been operated for

many years and the Commission has no plans to abolish it.

Compassion in World Farming believes that exports from the EC should be banned except to those countries which have standards of welfare during transport and at slaughter as high as those of the EC. Certainly no public subsidies should be paid to those engaging in so barbaric a trade. There can be few who wish to dig into their pockets to donate to this cruel cause.

Cruelty in Holland

A new film made by the Dutch Animal Welfare Society in 1993 portrays the transport of injured pigs and cattle in Holland. These are animals that should have been humanely slaughtered on the farm rather than being subjected to the rigours of transport to the slaughterhouse. The film shows animals which are unable to move being dragged off trucks, often by their ears or by chains attached to a rear leg. The animals are clearly in considerable distress.

Some are lame, others appear terribly deformed with their rear legs twisted at a hideous angle to their bodies. In the worst case a pig's inner organs have spilled out of its body – presumably through its anus. Still alive, it is being pushed and shoved forward.

At the slaughterhouse pigs are inefficiently stunned. Some need more than one application of the electrical tongs before being rendered unconscious. In some cases the tongs, instead of being applied to either side of the head, are placed one on top of the head and the other below the chin – this is completely the wrong position for the electrical tongs.

Pregnant cows

A new strand of the live trade has been developing during 1993. Holland appears to be the guilty party. In-calf heifers (pregnant cows) are being exported from Holland, through

Pregnant cows sent from Holland to the Republic of Ireland and Northern Ireland.

Britain, to the Republic of Ireland and Northern Ireland. These exports involve two sea crossings and three land journeys.

In the worst incident a ferry carrying 38 pregnant cows arrived at the port of Harwich on 10th June, 1993. 20 of the cows were found to be dead on arrival. The animals appear to have suffocated due to faulty/inadequate ventilation.

This is only one of a wide range of abuses discovered by the British authorities. For example, in May a Dutch truck transported pregnant cows from Holland to Northern Ireland. On arrival one heifer had to be put down immediately and several more had to be destroyed a few days later.

In February 1994 the Scottish Society for the Prevention of Cruelty to Animals urged the authorities to keep a close watch on calves being exported from Holland to Ireland through Stranraer, a port in south-west Scotland. Having endured this huge journey, many of the calves will be reared to adulthood in the Republic of Ireland and then exported live once more for slaughter in North Africa or the Middle East.[5]

Belgian abattoir

In July 1993, Compassion in World Farming gave a great deal of publicity to an investigation conducted by the leading Belgian animal welfare society Animaux en Péril at the slaughterhouse in Charleroi-Nord, Belgium. To their horror, Animaux en Peril found a sledgehammer being used in the slaughter of horses.

The horses were first stunned with a captive bolt pistol. They were then struck a massive blow on the head with a sledgehammer before their throats were cut.

Those horses which were properly stunned would not have felt the sledgehammer. Captive bolt stunning is, however, unlikely to be effective for each animal. Those horses which were not effectively stunned would have suffered considerably when being struck with the sledgehammer. The authorities tell us that this practice has now been stopped.

Compassion in World Farming petition

The public's increasing concern about the trade was highlighted by the fact that Compassion in World Farming's Ban Live Exports petition attracted almost 400,000 signatures.

On 15th September 1993, Penelope Keith, accompanied by Sir Richard Body MP (Con) and Labour's animal welfare spokesman Elliot Morley, handed in this massive petition to Agriculture Minister, Gillian Shephard MP.

Penelope Keith also handed over a shepherd's crook symbolising our wish that Mrs Shephard should be a 'good shepherd' and stop exporting British lambs, sheep and calves to Europe.

Commission's 1993 proposals

In August 1993 the Commission published proposed new rules under Article 13 of the 1991 EC Transport Directive.

The 1991 Directive only requires animals to be given food and water every 24 hours. This is clearly totally unsatisfactory.

The proposed new rules take the approach of providing different feeding and watering intervals and resting periods for each different species. Thus, under the rules, calves would have to be given food and water every 8 hours and horses every 6 hours. Adult cattle would have to be given water every 16 hours, but food only every 24 hours. Pigs would have to be given water every 8 hours but food only every 24 hours. The proposed new rules contrast with the position under UK law under which animals have to be given food and water every 15 hours.

Proposals will fail to halt trade

Article 13 of the 1991 Directive allows the Commission to propose 'maximum journey times'. This gives them the power to suggest a rule that animals should not be transported for more than a certain number of hours after which the journey must come to an end. The essential point of such a maximum journey time is that the journey could not be started up again even after the animals had been given food, water and rest.

The crucial defect of the Commission's proposals is that they have chosen not to propose any maximum journey limit. Instead they have just tinkered at the edges of the problem, suggesting a little improvement here and a minor tweak there. In short, the Commission's new rules will not really do anything to stop the suffering inherent in the live trade. And at this stage it is worth emphasising the sheer scale of the live trade. In 1992, 4,831,000 sheep and goats were transported between EC Member States. The figure for pigs was 8,993,000 and for cattle (adults and calves) it was 3,209,000.[6]

Chapter Twelve

The Economics of the Live Trade

It has for years been argued that from a humanitarian point of view the export of live animals should be replaced by the export of carcases. So what are the factors which continue to make the live trade economically attractive?

The reasons behind it vary from time to time and country to country; the common theme, however, is one of financial advantage to exporter and importer. Clearly no one engages in a trade unless they believe a profit can be made.

For it to be profitable to export live animals, a dealer must know that he can sell the animals in Europe for a price higher than the combined cost of:

a) what it costs him to buy the animals in the UK, plus

b) the cost of transporting them to Europe.

Moreover, the dealer is unlikely to export the live animals unless he knows the profit he can make is greater than the profit available from selling them to a UK abattoir.

For example, in 1989, a trade representative was quoted as saying: 'We could get a consignment of 600 lambs to Italy for £5 a head, giving the farmer a premium of £3 a lamb over the price he would get at a UK abattoir'.[1]

Finally, a dealer is unlikely to export the animals live if he will make a greater profit by exporting them as carcases.

Sheep are by far the largest component of British live exports. Of some 2 million animals exported in 1992, 1.3 million were sheep and lambs. France is the major destination for UK live sheep exports, with over one million being sent there in 1992.[2] In percentage terms, 83% of British live sheep exports went to France in 1992, with the remainder of the sheep going to Belgium (6%), the Republic of Ireland (5%), Holland (3%) and Germany (3%).

Price premium for 'home killed'

The French and other EC countries want British lamb, but often they prefer it live so that it can be sold as 'locally killed'. Just as New Zealand and British lamb are not regarded as identical products by British consumers (home killed lamb generally fetches a higher price than New Zealand lamb), so domestic lamb can be sold for more on the French market than the imported product.

Imported British lambs, slaughtered in French slaughter-houses, are sometimes marketed within France as domestically produced. As such they attract a price premium, French consumers being willing to pay more for a French product.

Put simply, the French meat trade likes to import live lamb because it can be passed off to the unsuspecting French consumer as French lamb, if it comes from a French abattoir. Sheep slaughtered in France are stamped with a French abattoir meat inspection stamp, whereas sheep imported as carcases will bear a UK abattoir stamp.

Recent research in two areas of France has shown that over half the lambs sold as 'Agneaux des bergers de France' or 'L'agneau francais' were in fact imported from Britain, the Netherlands or Poland.[3]

Professor Christopher Ritson has concluded that:

the main reason sustaining the export trade in live sheep is that exporting live rather than dead allows the product to attract a higher price on the French market, because it achieves the domestically killed price premium. This premium is sufficient to cover the extra costs for exporting live.[4]

Extra costs of exporting live

Exporting live animals is considerably more expensive than exporting carcases. It costs on average four times more to transport a live animal abroad than to transport a carcase. A number of factors are responsible for this.

A given vehicle can carry less live sheep than carcases, thereby increasing the transport costs for live animals. Ferry costs are higher for livestock vehicles. Moreover, refrigerated vehicles that carry carcases can often find return loads of meat or other produce, whereas livestock vehicles usually have to come back empty as the UK imports relatively few live animals.[5]

The cost of transporting live sheep from the UK to northern France is about £4.50 per head. This compares with a cost of about 90p for transporting a carcase over the same distance. It costs £6.25 to transport a live sheep to southern France, but only £1.20 to send a carcase.[6]

Looked at from the point of view of the cost of a kilogram of meat, it costs about 20p per kilogram more to transport live animals (rather than carcases) to northern France. This extra cost, however, is more than offset by the fact that the live animals may be sold as 'French produced' lamb which fetches 26p per kilogram more than imported meat. The extra cost of transporting live to southern France is about 28p per kilogram, but there, French produced lamb makes an extra 50p per kilogram.[7]

From the above it is clear that it is the willingness of French consumers to pay extra for a French product that makes it profitable to export live lambs despite the much higher cost of transporting live animals rather than carcases.

The French authorities have said that the practice of selling British lambs as French meat is illegal and that companies which would appear to have misled consumers would be prosecuted. A French embassy spokesman admitted, however, that there could be a problem with store lambs (animals which instead of being slaughtered straight away are kept for a period of further fattening). If such lambs are held for a particular time on a French farm they become regarded as French and may be legitimately sold as French lamb when they are slaughtered. About half the roughly 2 million lambs exported live from the UK to France in 1993 were such store lambs.[8]

Demand from French abattoirs

Any abattoir must kill a certain number of animals over a given period if it is to cover its capital and running costs. An abattoir experiencing a declining throughput must take steps to reverse the situation.

The number of lambs being reared in France has been falling sharply (by over 30% over the last decade),[9] and, as a result, French abattoirs are suffering from chronic overcapacity. In order to address this problem they are importing additional lambs to maintain their throughputs.

It has even been estimated that some five million lambs could be exported live from the UK by 1995. This prediction is based on the expectation that the French flock will continue to decline and that French abattoirs will continue to be able to recoup the additional costs of importing live animals from the premium paid by retailers for 'home killed' lamb.[10]

The position has been summarised by European AgriBusiness:

> The continuing contraction of the French flock, a major market for the UK, should ensure that demand for both meat and live lambs remains strong.[11]

It is not only French abattoirs that suck in British lambs. Abattoirs in the Irish Republic are importing pigs. Exports of live pigs from the UK reached 284,000 in the first nine months of 1992, double the same period in 1991. The Irish Republic imported 75% of these. The strong demand in the Republic comes from a small number of highly specialised abattoirs that need more pigs for slaughter than can be obtained domestically.[12]

Home cuts

Often we are told that animals must be exported live because different countries have their own preferred way of cutting the carcase.

On examination this argument proves to be a red herring. Carcases of animals slaughtered in the UK do not have to be cut before export. The whole carcase can be exported, leaving the importer to cut it according to local practice.

Alternatively, UK abattoirs are quite capable of cutting carcases to the specification required by the importing country.

Fresh meat

Another familiar refrain is: consumers abroad insist on freshly killed meat. In fact, modern technology permits the rapid transport of chilled meat throughout the Community. Freezing is not necessary for transport from one part of the EC to another; chilling is enough. Few people can tell the difference between chilled and freshly killed meat.

Adverse impact in UK of live exports

On a number of occasions the Meat Trades Journal, the meat trade's weekly, has highlighted the damaging impact in the UK of live exports.

As has been seen, French abattoirs have addressed their difficulties by importing live lambs. Their action has simply served to bequeath the problem of falling throughputs to British slaughterhouses.

UK lamb slaughtering dropped by 10% in May 1993, according to Ministry of Agriculture figures. These show that only 909,000 sheep and lambs were killed as compared with 1,223,000 in May 1992.

Many in the trade attribute the fall in UK slaughterings to increasing live exports which are reducing the number of animals available for UK abattoirs to kill.[13]

Slaughterers are deeply concerned. Dennis Knight from the Sims Group has blamed some abattoir closures on diverted throughput and has called for live exports to be banned.[14] The sight of Compassion in World Farming and the meat trade fighting side by side to halt live exports is, to say the least, somewhat unexpected.

Mr Knight added:

> All the abattoirs in the UK have spent millions of pounds so that they comply with EC [meat hygiene] regulations. The only way that the abattoirs can survive in business is to have full throughput. The more sheep that are exported live, the less chance there is of this happening.[15]

The problem of insufficient animals has been exacerbated by an increase in sheep and lamb prices. Here too live exports are the underlying factor. Competitive pressure from dealers wishing to export is pushing up live lamb prices.

David Maunder of Lloyd Maunders has been quoted as saying that the situation has become serious for slaughterers, with margins low and volumes significantly down.[16]

Moreover, the resultant high prices in the shops are driving consumers away to such an extent that the trade is now concerned that people may lose the taste for lamb.[17]

These problems have been mirrored in Denmark. A steep increase in Danish exports of live cattle to Germany has caused a decline in killings in Denmark. As a result, two slaughterhouses have closed. The director of the Danish Meat and Livestock Commission is most concerned at the prospect of Denmark exporting an increasing number of cattle instead of creating added value by processing beef in Denmark.[18]

The increasing volume of live calf exports from the UK has been causing problems similar to those emanating from the export of live lambs. High cattle prices in the UK and insufficient animals for domestic slaughterers have been the inevitable consequence of the export of some 420,000 young calves to France and Holland in 1992.[19]

The consumption of veal has been falling in Europe. However, despite this the demand for calves from the UK has increased because the supply of suitable calves from other sources has been falling. Most calves reared for veal are the bull calves of dairy cows. Dairy cow numbers have been falling in the EC due to milk quotas with the result that fewer calves are being born. Moreover, calf imports from eastern Europe have been disrupted due to animal health problems and the war in the former Yugoslavia.[20] These factors have led to an increased demand for calves from the UK and the Republic of Ireland. The strength of the demand is illustrated by the fact that in 1993 Holland imported 11% more calves than in 1992 (this figure refers to imports from all countries, not just from the UK).[21]

Price differentials have also been significant. In autumn 1993 veal calves were fetching £195-£235 a head on the continent compared with just £165 in Britain. This led to continental buyers being eager to buy at British markets.[22]

Referring to the fall in UK cattle slaughterings, the *Meat Trades Journal* has written:

Abattoirs blame calf exports which have regularly been over 400,000 head a year, the equivalent of ten weeks slaughterings at current throughput levels. Several abattoir owners claim the veal trade to France and the Netherlands is bleeding their industry dry.[23]

One industry spokesman has been quoted as saying:

Calves are the seed corn of our future and if they are exported live we can't process them. The industry is alarmed about the depth of leakage which is estimated at the equivalent of the throughput of ten large abattoirs.[24]

Indeed live exports have been identified by the President of the National Federation of Meat Traders as one of the principal causes of concern for the meat trade. He has written that 'jobs, profits and businesses throughout the meat trade in this country are in jeopardy'.[25]

In the future the problem may not be confined to sheep and calf exports. At present, because of BSE fears, there is a prohibition on the export of live adult cattle from the UK to the rest of the EC. Cattle breeders, however, hope that these restrictions will eventually be lifted, perhaps as early as 1995. Once they are removed, a considerable demand for live British cattle is expected. This, just like the export of live sheep and calves, will put fresh pressure on beleaguered British abattoirs. Indeed the secretary of the National Cattle Breeders' Association has been quoted as saying:

> We anticipate objections from abattoirs which are threatened with reduced throughput but we see live exports as a means of raising farm incomes.[26]

In July 1993 in the House of Commons, the Junior Agriculture Minister, Nicholas Soames MP, praised the role of the live export trade, stressing that it is worth £160 million per annum. He added that Europeans want animals to be slaughtered on the Continent because of their preference for their own countries' butchers' cuts.

In so speaking, Mr Soames brought down on his head the wrath of the meat trade. They were angry that the Minister, in praising live exports, had dismissed the disastrous effect they have on the slaughtering sector as a 'regrettable side effect'. The rift on live exports between farmers (who often support the live trade) and the meat trade was highlighted in a *Meat Trades Journal* editorial which said that the fact that the Minister went so far in defending live exports was proof that 'the interests of the farming lobby still appear to be paramount'.[27] They added that British farmers should support the domestic market 'in the interest of British jobs and adequate supplies of reasonably priced meat in British shops'.

At a time of high unemployment the point about jobs is an important one. Not only do live exports reduce the number of jobs available in British abattoirs, they also decrease employment in allied processing industries using offals, hides and skins. Put simply, if live animals are exported rather than being slaughtered in the UK, fewer hides and skins are available for use by the UK leather industry.

The *Meat Trades Journal* was particularly scathing about Mr Soames' remarks on European butchers' cuts, branding them an insult to the British meat trade and adding:

Does he not believe that British butchers can cut meat in the Continental style or to a particular specification?

Finally, we need to look at the Minister's statement that live exports are worth £160 million. At first sight this may appear to be an impressive contribution to the UK's trading position. However, as has been seen earlier, the UK imports much more meat than it exports.

Thus in 1992 the UK imported £2,033 million worth of meat and meat products. If rather than being exported animals had been slaughtered for home consumption, the UK's imports bill could have been reduced. Indeed, slaughtering at home would have led to bigger savings on imports than losses on exports. This is because if kept in the UK, some of the animals would have been fattened before slaughter thereby increasing their value by the time they got to slaughter age.

In conclusion it can be seen that live exports fail to make economic sense, leading to reduced throughputs for UK abattoirs (and even to abattoir closures), reduced employment in the slaughtering and processing sectors and higher prices for UK consumers.

It should also be stressed that the majority of exports are in the form of meat. The red meat export trade was worth £630 million in 1992 (live exports being worth £160 million).[28] In other words some 80% of exports were in the form of carcases in 1992. Given that live exports are impossible to justify on welfare grounds, surely the time has come for all exports to be in carcase form. Sadly, some sectors of the trade predict that the proportion of exports which are live will see an increase over the next few years.

Chapter Thirteen

The Live Trade Blues: Late 1993 and 1994

The Blues are the sound of plaint, but also of complaint. The sound of sadness but also of protest and anger.

So too was it with the live trade in 1993 and 1994. Sadness as the scale of the trade grew, anger as its sufferings became clearer, but also determination that this should not be, that this should be ended.

Prince Sadruddin Aga Khan

One person determined to speak out was Prince Sadruddin Aga Khan. Towards the end of 1992 he saw Compassion in World Farming's video *The Road to Misery* on French television. He was deeply disturbed by what he saw.

In the following months he gathered together some of Europe's leading animal welfare groups and formed a new coalition called the European Committee for Improvements in the Transport of Farm Animals.

At the new Committee's Brussels launch on 21st September 1993, Prince Sadruddin declared:

> The cruelties associated with the transport of live farm animals across Europe are scandalous. How can the perpetration of such atrocities continue to be tolerated in a society which considers itself to be civilised?

A new Manifesto was unveiled at the launch listing the Committee's demands. This principally calls for animals to be slaughtered near the farm, and in particular urges the adoption of a maximum limit of 8 hours on the journeys of animals being transported for slaughter. The plan was to invite celebrities and opinion formers throughout Europe to endorse the Manifesto. The first signature: that of Brigitte Bardot, at the Brussels Press Conference.

The Manifesto's UK launch followed on 1st December 1993 at a Press Conference organised by Compassion in World Farming and the RSPCA, both founder members of the new coalition.

Princess Catherine, the Prince's wife, spoke eloquently at the launch of the misery engendered by the live trade. In the UK the Manifesto has been signed by a range of parliamentarians and celebrities including Julie Christie, Dame Judi Dench, Joanna Lumley, Martin Shaw, Katie Boyle and Peter O'Sullevan.

Behind the scenes the Prince worked tirelessly, writing to and meeting MEPs and the Agriculture Ministers of the European Union's Member States. (On 1st November 1993 the Maastricht Treaty came into force and the European Community became known as the European Union (EU); it still, however, continues often to be referred to as the 'European Community'.) Undoubtedly the Prince's involvement gave fresh heart and impetus to the campaign. He brought with him an exceptional record as an international statesman and campaigner on environmental issues.

In 1977 the Prince founded the Bellerive Foundation which has established a worldwide reputation as one of the leading action groups promoting conservation of nature and natural resources, as well as respect for all forms of life. The Bellerive Foundation has been elected to the Global 500 Honour Roll of the United Nations' Environment Programme for 'outstanding practical achievements in the protection and improvement of the environment'.

Importation of disease

The introduction of the Single Market on 1st January 1993 brought with it the free movement of animals throughout the European Community. For a long time some had been warning that a single European market with no border controls would make it easier for animal diseases to be passed from one country to another.

These fears were smoothly assuaged by officialdom who assured us that all was under control. They explained that before the start of a journey, livestock would be inspected by a vet to ensure that they were free of disease and a veterinary certificate would be issued. The importing country would have to rely on that certificate and could no longer insist on quarantine for imported livestock.

Before the year was out the new arrangements were exposed as being unable to prevent the spread of animal diseases. The UK's health status was being jeopardised by the insistence on free movement without proper border controls. Diseases which were brought into Britain in 1993 by imported stock include warble fly infestation, brucellosis and equine viral arteritis (a disease affecting the arteries).

Prior to 1993 Britain had managed to eradicate warble fly, which attacks cattle. The warble fly lays its eggs on the animals' legs. Once the eggs have hatched, the larvae enter the cattle, spending the winter in the gullet or spinal cord. In the spring the warble larvae emerge from the back, having caused swelling under the skin.[1] Warble fly causes severe discomfort and loss of condition.

In 1989 there had been two warble fly outbreaks in Britain, with one in 1990 and none in both 1991 and 1992. By November 1993, however, 107 herds had been affected.[2] These outbreaks were traced to cattle imported from France.

Indeed, 221 cattle imported from France between January and July 1993 proved to be infested with warble fly. Between April and July, 39 farms were placed under movement restrictions as a result of the warble outbreak and 1,490 farms were served treatment notices imposing movement controls pending treatment against warble fly.[3]

The dismantling of border controls appears also to have led to the re-emergence in Britain of brucellosis. This chronic disease can be transmitted to people either by contact with an infected animal or by drinking non-pasteurised contaminated milk.

Brucellosis had previously been eradicated in Britain. During 1993, however, there were outbreaks of brucellosis in cattle on a Cheshire farm and two Anglesey farms. These outbreaks were associated with an animal imported from France. In response, the government stepped up brucellosis checks on cattle imported from France and Holland.

Referring to the attacks of warble fly and brucellosis, the Farming News warned of the 'health hazard posed to millions of domestic and farm animals from the unrestricted import of unhealthy animals'.[4]

Just four months into the new regime, foot and mouth disease appeared in Italy, apparently brought in by animals from eastern Europe.

Closer to home, some 249 cattle from eastern Europe ended up illegally in the UK and reacted positively to foot and mouth tests.[5] This does not necessarily mean that they have the disease, but rather that they have been vaccinated against it.

At first sight this may not appear to present a problem, but it does. Vaccinated animals can carry the foot and mouth virus without showing clinical signs of the disease. Moreover, in the UK and the rest of the European Union there is a policy not of vaccinating against foot and mouth but of eradicating it by slaughtering infected animals. If there was an outbreak of foot and mouth in the UK, the presence of vaccinated animals would mean that when animals reacted positively to tests, the authorities would not know if they actually had the disease or whether they had been vaccinated.

In conclusion, the abolition of border controls is not just a welfare disaster; it also facilitates the spread of animal diseases. Indeed, this issue generated so much concern that in March 1994 the House of Commons Agriculture Committee announced that it was to hold an inquiry into the system of health controls on the importation of live animals. The Committee announced that it was particularly interested in the effectiveness of health controls on the importation of farm livestock originating from other EU Member States and from non-EU countries.

New hopes and old fears

As we have already seen, in August 1993 the European Commission published proposed new rules on transport. Whilst containing some welcome measures, these simply did not go far enough. In particular, they failed to propose a maximum limit on slaughter journeys. Such a limit, if sufficiently short, would effectively shift the live trade into a carcase trade.

In the autumn attention turned to the European Parliament who were due to consider the proposed new rules. David Morris MEP was again appointed as Rapporteur as he had been on this subject in 1990. He produced an excellent Report which, amongst other things, called for a maximum limit of 8 hours on slaughter journeys. In December the Report was adopted by the Parliament. What was extraordinary was the margin of the vote. 271 votes for the Report and just 6 against.

Now surely the democratic voice would be heeded. Not so. As we have seen before, the Council of Ministers is perfectly happy to ignore the wishes of the Parliament, despite its being the only one of the EU institutions to be democratically elected.

And yet there were some hopeful signs. In Council discussions on the proposed new rules, Germany, supported by Denmark and Holland, was pressing for the imposition of a maximum journey limit. The UK government, despite its claims to lead the way on welfare in Europe, was refusing to support the German proposal.

The UK argued that the problems could be solved by stipulating that animals must be given food and water every 15 hours. The trouble with this is that after being fed and watered the animals can be transported for a second, and even a third, period of 15 hours.

This approach can never have more than a marginal impact on the problem. The proper solution, as advocated by Germany, Holland, Denmark and the European Parliament is to impose an overall limit on slaughter journeys. That limit should at most be 8 hours. After that time animals would have to have reached the slaughterhouse. There could be no extension of the journey.

Without British support the German proposal was unlikely to get very far. They needed the backing of one of the other big EU countries. Only Germany, the UK, France and Italy have 10 votes in the Council. France and Italy were unlikely to support a welfare proposal. But if the UK were to join forces with Germany, then there would be some real weight behind a proposal which could usher in the end of long distance live transport.

But the British Minister, Gillian Shephard, refused to budge. What was particularly galling was her insistence on having her cake and eating it. She put out a press release claiming that 'Britain takes the lead in animal welfare in Europe' while at the same time blocking any real progress by her refusal to support the German proposal.

Throughout the autumn of 1993 the British public placed enormous pressure on the Minister in an effort to win her over to the need for radical change. All to no avail. She remained unmoved.

Then in February 1994 there was a new flood of public pressure, a mixture of concern for the animals and indignation at government inaction. This new wave was generated by a Press Conference held by Joanna Lumley and Compassion in World Farming, which was followed the next day by a powerful *World in Action* television programme.

A Compassion in World Farming video shown at the Press Conference revealed how tiny calves, many just a few days old, are shipped off to continental veal crate farms. The crate is so narrow that the calves cannot even turn round. This system is illegal in the UK and yet 1,000 calves are exported each day to these 'living coffins' in Holland and France.

The video also showed scenes of horrendous cruelty in Spanish slaughterhouses. Sheep were seen being shackled to a rail by one hind leg. No attempt was made to stun them.

Hanging upside down, their throats were cut and they bled to death whilst fully conscious.

Clearly shaken by the video, Joanna Lumley told the audience:

> We breed these animals. Their lives and deaths are our responsibility. It is simply unacceptable to treat living creatures in this way.

Joanna and Compassion in World Farming also used the press conference to announce the launch of a new campaign. Jointly they had produced a postcard calling on the Agriculture Minister to end the cruel live trade. Joanna urged everyone who supported the campaign to sign one of these cards so that later in the year she could deliver a huge shoal of them to the Minister to underscore the strength of public opposition to live exports.

The next morning nearly every newspaper in the land carried major stories highlighting the campaign and Joanna's plea for a ban on live exports.

That evening Granada Television's *World in Action* broadcast a hard-hitting exposé called 'Animal Traffic'. Using some of Compassion in World Farming's footage, and with extensive interviews with the author, it revealed the suffering inherent in the trade. A massive 5.8 million people watched the programme.

One revelation was particularly surprising. When in January 1993 the government announced that they were going to allow animals to be sent to Spain for slaughter, they gave a firm assurance that UK animals would only go to abattoirs guaranteed by the Spanish government to be complying with the EC Directive requiring animals to be stunned before slaughter.

During the programme *World in Action* revealed a leaked letter from the government's Chief Veterinary Officer. This showed that the government had been failing to implement its assurance. The letter, dated November 1993, referred to the fact that one Ministry Division had received three applications for permission to send animals to Spain for slaughter. The first thing officials should have checked is that the applicant was sending the animals to an abattoir on the list of those complying with the EC stunning law.

In two cases the exporters named abattoirs not on that list. Officials failed to spot this and let the animals go to Spain. In the third case no abattoir was named let alone one on the approved list. Again officials failed to spot this and again animals were allowed to go to Spain in breach of the government's assurance.

Nor were the problems confined to animals going to Spain. British exporters had always liked to suggest that all the difficulties lay abroad, with continental traders and hauliers being the ones who broke the laws on feeding and watering, etc. In 1994 it became increasingly clear that this was simply not the case.

The World in Action programme trailed a British exporter who took his animals all the way from Somerset to southern France. During the 28 hour journey the animals were not once given food and water. This was in breach of the 1991 EC Directive's rule that they must be given food and water at least every 24 hours and the British rule that they must be fed and watered every 15 hours. (Ministry lawyers take the view that Britain's 15 hour rule in the Welfare of Animals During Transport Order 1992 applies to journeys starting in Britain even if the animals have left this country by the time the 15 hour point is reached.)

Nor was this an isolated case. During late 1993 and the early part of 1994 local County Councils (who have primary responsibility for enforcing animal transport legislation) together with the Ministry of Agriculture and the Department of Transport undertook a major investigation. This looked into allegations that a number of British exporters were flouting the laws designed to protect welfare during export journeys.[7] At the time of writing (June 1994) charges had been brought against British exporters, haulage companies and lorry drivers for alleged breaches of the laws designed to protect animal health and welfare during transport. Other prosecutions were in the pipeline.

Importation of diseased sheep from Poland and Spain

Things reached the height of absurdity when, in early 1994, Britain began to import live sheep from Poland and Spain for slaughter in Birmingham. It makes little sense for a country which exports some 5,000 live sheep each day to be at the very same time engaged in importing live sheep.

A consignment of 200 sheep arrived from Spain at Christmas 1993. Then in the first three months of 1994 four consignments of sheep arrived from Poland with a further four coming from Spain.

There were major problems with the second consignment from Poland. Thirty of the sheep were condemned as unfit for human consumption after being slaughtered at a Birmingham halal abattoir. Several of these sheep had caseous lymphadenitis, a severe infection of the lymph nodes. The Environmental Services Department of Birmingham City Council reported that 'these abscesses were found throughout the carcasses and also in the organs and offal of the sheep causing them to be totally condemned on inspection'.[8]

Caseous lymphadenitis is virtually unheard of in Britain and its spread into the British flock would be a major blow. Again, it is clear that a serious threat is posed to the health of UK farm animals by the EU's insistence that border controls cannot be allowed to impede the trade in live animals. The President of the Sheep Veterinary Society was quoted as saying:

People are jeopardising the efforts that have been made to keep disease out of this island and it is absolutely ridiculous to sacrifice all this on the whim of free trade.[9]

Some of the animals arriving in this consignment from Poland were found to be suffering from arthritis, lameness and swollen feet, which are thought to have been caused by lengthy periods of confinement. Two sheep were dead on arrival in Dover, one died in the pens in Birmingham, and four remained in Kent as they were judged unfit to travel.[10]

In the wake of the Chernobyl disaster in the mid-1980's there was concern as to whether Polish animals could be contaminated with radiation and thus whether the meat was safe to eat. Tests were carried out and proved to be negative.

One consignment of sheep from Spain included seventeen animals which had to be condemned as unfit for human consumption. Shockingly, one ewe in one of the Spanish consignments gave birth to a lamb in the slaughterhouse lairage.[11] This ewe should never have been sent from Spain as Directive 91/628/EEC expressly prohibits the transport of 'pregnant animals likely to give birth during carriage' (paragraph 1 of Chapter 1 of the Directive's Annex).

The grim tale continued with the arrival of a fourth consignment from Poland on 17th March 1994. Two sheep were dead on arrival with twelve being unfit for human consumption. All were dirty and tired.[12]

Councillor Bryan Bird, Deputy Leader of Birmingham City Council, issued a press statement making it clear that he wanted to see the government and the EU 'take action to end the misery of hundreds of animals who are dragged all the way across Europe'.[13]

The final consignment from Spain arrived in Poole on 22nd March. One sheep was found to be dead on arrival with another three having to be put down. One ewe had given birth during the journey. The animals were held overnight for a veterinary examination the following day, by which time a second sheep had lambed. The examination found 26 sheep to be unfit to continue their journey to the Birmingham abattoir. They were destroyed. So too were the new-born lambs and their mothers.[14]

The cycle continues

Throughout the first half of 1994 the cruelty and absurdity of the live trade continued to be highlighted by new incidents and fresh revelations.

In February sixteen cows died on two separate flights into Britain from Toronto, Canada. (Each year hundreds of pedigree cattle are flown from Canada to Britain). Post-mortems found the animals died of suffocation. A Ministry of Agriculture official was quoted as saying that the likely cause of death was 'too many animals and not enough air'.[15]

On 25th April, thirty-nine sheep being exported from Britain to France died during the overnight ferry crossing from Portsmouth to Le Havre.[16] Subsequently it was revealed that the previous week thirty sheep had died during a Channel crossing. No cause of death was established by the authorities.

At the same time allegations began to emerge that UK cattle were being sent illegally across the border from Northern Ireland to the Republic of Ireland and that some of these animals were then being exported live to the Middle East and North Africa.[17] If these allegations are true, it means that UK cattle are being subjected to the misery of long sea journeys (ten days and sometimes considerably more) and a painful death at their destination where they will be slaughtered without first being stunned. (Further details of these allegations may be found in Chapter 14 on the Irish trade.)

An answer to a Parliamentary Question in April revealed a curious state of affairs. It stated that in the previous twelve months 178 animals had been dead and 352 recumbent on arrival at a particular Birmingham slaughterhouse ('recumbent' means unable to get up through injury or disease).[18]

What was extraordinary was that not one single prosecution had been brought in respect of any one of those 530 animals. Now when an animal is dead or recumbent on arrival at the slaughterhouse, there must, in many cases, be a reasonable likelihood that it was unfit to travel in the first place. And it is an offence to transport an unfit animal (Welfare of Animals during Transport Order 1992). It is hard to imagine why the authorities (the local Council and the Ministry of Agriculture) did not think any one of these 530 cases worthy of prosecution.

How many animals are being exported from the UK? No one knows. Certainly not the Ministry of Agriculture. In March, in answer to a Parliamentary Question, Nicholas

Soames MP (Parliamentary Secretary at the Ministry) said 'details of the total numbers of live animals exported in 1993 are not yet available. It is not possible to say when they will become available'.[19]

In previous years, the figures were published soon after the year's end. They were collected at the port lairages where, before the sea journey to the continent, animals were by law rested and inspected by a vet. With the end of compulsory lairaging in 1993 seems to have gone the ability to collect clear statistics as to the number of animals being exported. Certainly at the time of writing (June 1994) the Ministry has still not produced any figures for 1993.

Amidst the gloom generated by these tales of suffering and official complacency, there were heartening developments abroad. Earlier in the year Austria passed a law limiting slaughter journeys to six hours and a distance of 150 km (or 300 km on major roads). This shows that it can be done; a country can choose to put an end to long-distance live transport. The new law comes into force in 1995. Sadly, if Austria joins the EU, it may well find itself pressurised to abandon this measure in the interests of the famous level playing field – and a pretty muddy, low-lying field it is.

Then in May the German Parliament passed a resolution calling on the German government to press for an 8-hour journey limit during the Brussels negotiations. This was a welcome confirmation of Germany's desire to see a firm limit placed on long distance transport.

The strength of public concern in Britain was highlighted when on 23rd May Joanna Lumley presented to the Agriculture Minister 50,000 postcards demanding an end to live exports.

At the same time Compassion in World Farming launched a new video entitled *For a Few Pennies More*. This shows the full horror of the transport of live animals across Europe and demonstrates that in some parts of the EU welfare standards during transport continue to be appallingly low. The film shows cattle being beaten at a French market; the brutal handling of tiny calves during unloading in Italy; and pigs too lame to walk being kicked and dragged to the slaughterhouse.

On launching their video investigation Compassion in World Farming again called for a ban on live exports, arguing that once animals leave the UK there is nothing the government can do to safeguard their welfare either during transport or at the slaughterhouse.

Recognising the vital importance of also making progress at the European level, Compassion in World Farming had earlier in the year helped to establish a French sister organisation 'Protection Mondiale des Animaux de Ferme' (PMAF). As much of the investigation had been shot in France, PMAF produced a French version of the film entitled *Pour Quelques Centimes de Plus*.

Throughout the early months of the year discussions between the EU Member States had rumbled on about the new transport ryules which the Commission had proposed in 1993 under Article 13 of the 1991 Transport Directive. Just as everyone thought that no decisions would be reached until the autumn, the matter was placed on the agenda for the meeting of the EU Council of Agriculture Ministers in Luxembourg on 20th June 1994.

What was on the table for decision was a very weak package proposed by the Greek Presidency. The package contained no maximum time limit on the journeys of animals being transported for slaughter and would have led to no significant improvements. Worst of all, the Greek proposals made no provision for a review of the situation until 1998. In effect, any hopes of progress would be squashed for four years.

Compassion in World Farming and others were eager for the Greek deal to be rejected. Germany, Holland and Denmark, all of whom were pressing for a maximum journey limit, could be relied on to vote against the Greek package. However, in the Council 23 votes are needed to block a proposal and those three countries had only 18 votes between them. The UK's 10 votes were crucial. If the UK were to line up with Germany, the Greek proposals could be rejected.

To their horror, however, animal welfare societies were

given to understand that the UK was prepared to support the Greek package. Immediately Compassion in World Farming and others launched a last minute campaign. Compassion in World Farming published advertisements in the *Independent*, *Times* and *Telegraph* saying to the UK Agriculture Minister 'If you sign (the Greek deal) – then resign'. Towards the end of Monday 20th June the news came through from Luxembourg. The UK had voted with Germany, Holland, Denmark and Belgium to reject the Greek package.

The animal welfare world had won a huge victory. We lived to fight another day. The Germans made it clear that they would try to make progress on securing a maximum journey limit during their Presidency (from 1st July 1994 to the end of the year). The UK Agriculture Minister, Gillian Shephard put out a press release saying she had obtained a commitment from the Commission to bring forward proposals on journey limits by 1st July 1995. It seemed that at last the UK had accepted the principle that there should be a maximum journey limit, although the depth of their commitment to this principle remained unclear.

All these, the victories, the set backs, the uncertainties are just drops in the ocean of time. Slowly humanity is learning to treat animals as beings with lives of their own, not as things placed in this world for us to use as we wish. Live exports and the long distance transport of animals will come to an end. Deep-down all that is being negotiated is the time-scale.

Chapter Fourteen

The Irish Trade

Mary - Anne Bartlett

The Republic of Ireland is a predominantly agricultural country with roots in agriculture and livestock trading which can be traced back to the seventeenth century. Indeed, agriculture is currently the Republic's largest industry with farm animals and animal products (mainly milk) being by far the largest agricultural sector. Sheep slightly outnumber cattle (8.7 million to 7 million in 1993), but cattle, both dairy and beef, are the principal farm animal in terms of value.[1]

With a human population currently under 4 million, the home market is inadequate to support such a high level of livestock production. For example in 1992, 81% of sheep were exported either live or as meat, with only 19% being used at home.[2] CBF (Irish Livestock and Meat Board) has said:

> The Irish livestock and meat industry is unique in its export orientation and dependence.[3]

Much of the export trade is in the form of meat and animal products. However, the number of animals exported live continues to be high; indeed, exports of live cattle doubled between 1992 and 1993.[4] While some animals are exported for breeding, the majority are destined for slaughter.

Table 1 shows the numbers of animals exported live from the Republic of Ireland over the past 5 years. The number of animals exported to destinations other than Northern Ireland is shown in brackets.

TABLE

Year	Cattle		Sheep & goats		Pigs	
	Total	Excluding N.Ireland	Total	Excluding N.Ireland	Total	Excluding N.Ireland
1993	370,000*	(330,000)*	no data		no data	
1992	186,443	(125,548)	305,196	(112,513)	150,817	(44,200)
1991	138,030	(52,460)	214,224	(116,502)	87,544	(3,906)
1990	184,855	(65,644)	243,137	(126,393)	51,351	(995)
1989	170,292	(50,155)	132,647	(32,927)	57,597	(362)

*estimated

Table: Numbers of live animals exported from the Republic of Ireland, 1989 to 1993.

Sources: Statistics for exports of live animals, CSO, Dublin, and 1993 Annual Review and Outlook, CBF (Irish Livestock and Meat Board).

Traditionally, Britain and Northern Ireland have been destinations for live animals travelling from the Republic of Ireland. For example, 74% of live cattle leaving the Republic in 1950 were destined for Great Britain, with 96% of live sheep and 89% of live pigs going to Northern Ireland. Though trade to Britain has diminished, cross-border trade continues, with 71% of all live pigs and 63% of live sheep going to Northern Ireland in 1992.[5] Whereas Northern Ireland was the most popular destination for live cattle over the past decade, numbers have been steadily declining in recent years, with 1993 seeing the lowest figure yet at just 40,000 head.[6] CBF (Irish Livestock and Meat Board) suggests that this downward trend reflects a strengthening meat export industry in the Republic.[7]

With the opening of EU markets, Irish animals are increasingly being exported long distances to continental European Union (EU) countries. Live sheep and lambs go mainly to France and Spain,[8] with young calves being sent to Holland and France, where most will end up in cruel veal crate farms.[9] There have also been some suggestions that Irish calves are being taken overland to Eastern Europe to replace stock which have been devastated by disease, though this has not been officially confirmed.[10]

Due to Ireland's geographical location, live animals exported to other EU destinations (except Northern Ireland) face at least one sea crossing, and often a lengthy overland journey as well. For example, sheep may be taken by road from an Irish farm or market to Rosslare, a south coast port. From there they go by sea to Cherbourg or Le Havre in northern France. The long journey to a slaughterhouse or farm in France, Spain or Italy is completed by road.

1993 saw the number of live cattle exported from the Republic of Ireland rise dramatically from 186,443 in 1992 to approximately 370,000.[11] Most of this increase was due to the re-opening of markets in North Africa and the Middle East. These had been closed due to fears of BSE ('mad cow disease') and the Gulf War. BSE fears were stemmed by the Republic of Ireland's good health status and strict BSE controls which include a policy of slaughtering the whole herd if one animal is found to be infected. In 1993, exports to countries outside the EU accounted for about 62% of total cattle exports, with Egypt and Libya the main markets, taking 170,000 and 40,000 cattle respectively.[12] Exporters who send cattle to countries outside the EU receive generous subsidies from the taxpayer to reward them for not adding to the EU's vast mountain of unwanted beef.

Welfare problems

It is difficult to get information about the welfare aspects of the Irish trade in live animals. Though the Department of Agriculture, Food and Forestry expresses the view that it is in the trade's economic interest to deliver animals to their destination in good condition[13], specific questions go unanswered. Statistics showing injuries and mortalities of animals in transit appear to be unobtainable. Even information about how this trade is monitored in Ireland is very limited. It is only from other sources that we know of some incidents and prosecutions involving Irish animals.

For example, when Greenore Port (which ships cattle to North Africa and the Middle East) was temporarily closed in March 1994 by the Department of Agriculture, Food and Forestry – ostensibly for animal welfare reasons[14] –

Compassion in World Farming asked for details. None were forthcoming, and a Department official explained that: 'The Department's dealings with individuals or companies are confidential and therefore I will not be disclosing any details of our communications with the authorities for Greenore Port . . .'.[15]

In August 1992, a champion cattle breeder described to a local newspaper how starved and stressed heavily pregnant heifers were being shipped from the Continent to Ireland in appalling conditions. The animals were overcrowded and given little food or water. Some went into premature labour, and he witnessed their dead calves being thrown overboard from the ferry between France and Rosslare.[16]

Less than a year later, in June 1993, UK authorities at Harwich checked a consignment of 38 pregnant heifers en route from Holland to Ireland. They found 20 animals dead from suffocation and heat exhaustion after being forced to spend eight hours in an unventilated truck.[17] Compassion in World Farming's request to Agricultural Minister Joe Walsh for a full enquiry received only a standard reply. The Department were reported as saying that such cases were the responsibility of the exporting country.[18]

At around the same time, pregnant heifers being imported into Ireland from the Continent gave birth immediately on landing at the quayside at Harwich. They were then forced to continue their journey to Ireland. Unfortunately, the UK authorities learned of the incident too late to act.

If transit conditions cannot even be controlled for valuable breeding animals – and these incidents show this is clearly the case – then animals destined for slaughter are likely to be treated with even less care.

Some prosecutions have ensued. For example, in June 1993, a driver carrying 260 calves from Ireland was stopped by British authorities at Dover. The animals had already travelled for some 26 hours without food, water or rest.[19] The driver was found to have no journey plan. This is a document detailing intended stops for feeding and watering animals in transit, and is a legal requirement under EU law for journeys over 24 hours in length. On inspection it was found that one calf had already died, and nine were unfit to travel any further. Prosecution was successful, with the driver being fined.

After the tragedy of the 20 dead pregnant heifers, the British Ministry of Agriculture, responsible for checking animals in transit through Britain, confirmed that there are concerns with animals travelling to and from the Republic of Ireland.[20] Now that border checks have been discontinued in the Single European Market, it is likely that problems with Irish animals will be even harder to detect.

Long sea journeys

It is difficult to obtain precise information as to the welfare of animals making long sea-journeys from Ireland for slaughter in the Middle East and North Africa, and again no mortality or injury figures appear to be available.

In the past, certain cases of cruelty have been brought to public attention. Two of the most notable are described below:

Siba Queen, December 1979

The *Siba Queen* was loaded in Cork with some 3,000 cattle due to sail to North Africa. The Cork Society for the Prevention of Cruelty to Animals (Cork SPCA) Inspector's Report described conditions on board:

> Apart from being overcrowded, the cattle were wet and shivering and standing in about six inches of liquid (urine and muck) ... A lot of them had injuries to legs and eyes ... Cattle on the lower decks, apart from standing in a liquid slurry, had urine seeping through from the top decks, both on to them and into what there was of feed and drink ... There was no ventilation in the lower decks, making it difficult to breathe ... Some of [the animals] had their heads and limbs jammed between the bars rendering them unable to move at all ...[21]

Miranda, **August 1981**

> This converted banana carrier was loaded with 1,763 cat-
> tle destined for Alexandria in Egypt. There were delays
> in leaving Waterford because a Department of
> Agriculture veterinary inspector was dissatisfied with
> the ship's ventilation system. On the voyage, further
> problems with the ventilation system arose, and also
> with the water supply. By the time the ship reached
> Alexandria, 722 of the animals had died in great distress
> from heat exhaustion and dehydration.[22] A spokesperson
> for the Department of Agriculture explained '... The
> ventilation system got clogged up and the animals suffo-
> cated ...'.[23]

It is generally felt that these two horrific cases have led to
improvements, and some of the livestock ships are now modern and purpose-built. Nonetheless, Compassion in World
Farming believes that such long sea journeys, by their very
nature, inflict great stress on the animals.

Animals travelling to countries in North Africa and the
Middle East will normally spend 8 to 10 days at sea, though
there are reports of sea-crossings to Libya being extended to
three weeks when gales are encountered.[24] Such sea journeys
can only be stressful to farm animals, especially in stormy conditions.

For example, in December 1989, there were reports of the *El
Novillo* en route from Ireland to Saudi Arabia with 1,200 cattle
on board floundering in stormy seas near the Scilly Isles. The
ship continued to sail into the wind, not trying to put ashore
until it finally docked in Italy and unloaded half the animals;
the rest continued the journey.[25] One can only imagine the conditions in the midst of such a storm, with more than a
thousand animals confined below decks on a ship being
tossed in heavy seas.

A trawler skipper from Waterford, in a letter to the Irish
Times, described vividly how cattle cannot be sick:

> They are ruminants and digest their food by fermenta-

tion. When they are exposed to extreme motion, the fermentation increases and the gas production in their stomachs becomes excessive, resulting in the condition known as bloat. The whole abdomen becomes grossly extended, they suffer acute pain, falling down on the floor as they are flung around from side to side, grinding their teeth, moaning and groaning in agony, unable to breathe properly until, after hours or days of the most terrible suffering, their hearts eventually give out and, mercifully, they die.[26]

Some of the problems inherent in this trade were highlighted in December 1993 when the a livestock boat carrying 1,200 cattle en route from Cork to Libya had to call into Brixham harbour (in Devon) for repairs. The cattle remained on board during the four-day delay while repairs were carried out. Even then the vessel's troubles were not over. Shortly after setting sail from Brixham, the Captain decided the weather was too bad to continue and he had to drop anchor in Tor Bay to ride out the storm.[27]

In addition to the problems of the long sea journeys, animals may be subjected to poor treatment in the countries of destination. Welfare conditions in these non-EU countries are beyond our legal jurisdiction and therefore totally outside our control. The following extract from a letter to the Irish Times illustrates this point; it was written after a visit on board a cattle ship in Waterford, and discussion with the ship's Captain:

[The Captain] said – and he stressed the words – that the suffering and cruelty start in Tripoli. Neither he nor the crew are allowed on shore but they can watch the unfortunate animals being beaten and crammed into lorries . . .[28]

Finally, after having survived the long and stressful sea-journey from Ireland, and the confusion and noise of loading and unloading, the animals will probably be killed without pre-slaughter stunning, suffering an agonising death by having their throats cut whilst fully conscious. It would clearly be much more humane to slaughter the animals in Ireland and export them in carcase form.

The Irish meat versus live exports debate

As in the UK, so in the Republic of Ireland the meat trade is deeply concerned about the impact of live exports. Every live animal leaving Ireland takes with it jobs in the slaughter and meat processing industries which would remain at home if the export trade was in meat. Estimates of jobs which will be lost in the Republic of Ireland as a result of the current high level of live cattle exports have been put at between 750[29] and 3,000[30], a significant number in view of the Republic of Ireland's low population and high unemployment figures.

The economic argument against exporting animals alive is certainly not a new one, as this excerpt from an analysis of exports from Waterford in 1932 illustrates:

The export of such live animals is not good economics. ... These animals are being turned into finished products in another country and so we lose the additional value that is added to them, thus leading to lessened employment of our people, and smaller use of the capital that is, or at least should be, readily available for this purpose. In addition, we lose their valuable by-products on which an entire monograph could be easily written.[31]

When the numbers of live cattle exported from Ireland doubled from 186,443 in 1992 to about 370,000 in 1993 (due mainly to the major resumption of the live cattle trade to Libya and Egypt), it is not surprising that the meat versus live exports debate came to the fore again. People began questioning the economic wisdom of exporting large numbers of cattle whilst Irish meat factories claimed they were being starved of their raw material, as did the hide industry in Waterford [32] and the Federation of Irish Renderers.[33]

In 1994, Agricultural Minister Joe Walsh was quoted as saying that jobs and investment in the meat industry were being jeopardised by the current high level of live exports,[34] although he has also said that live exports are crucial to maintain general competitiveness.[35] Meanwhile, the meat factories claimed that EU subsidies for live cattle destined for non-EU countries had weighted the trade unfairly in favour of live exports.[36]

During 1994, the meat versus live exports debate has heated up. Various controversies have emerged, with accusations from both sides of 'dirty tricks'.[37]

When Greenore Port (used to ship cattle out to the Middle East and North Africa) was temporarily closed by Department of Agriculture officials in March 1994, ostensibly for animal welfare inadequacies [38], it was widely believed that the closure was in reality to allow more cattle to reach Irish meat factories.[39]

The most serious allegation to emerge (in April 1994) is that over the past year some 50,000 UK cattle had been illegally smuggled across the border from Northern Ireland into the Republic[40] (exports of live cattle over 6 months old from the UK to the rest of the EU are prohibited as a protective measure against the spread of BSE). The suspicion is that while some of these cattle originate in Northern Ireland, others have been bought in Scotland or England, shipped from Stranraer (Scotland) to Larne (Northern Ireland) and from there sent unlawfully to the Republic.[41]

The alleged motive lies in the serious shortage of cattle in the Republic, a shortage arising partly as a result of the surge in live exports to the Middle East and North Africa. The suggestion is that Irish traders have been importing live cattle from the UK to help them meet export orders to the EU and to the Middle East and North Africa.[42]

For UK dealers the alleged attraction of the trade is that it allows them to circumvent the ban on the export of adult cattle to the rest of the EU and indeed to those other countries which have prohibited the import of UK live cattle.[43]

These allegations are potentially damaging to the reputation of both the Irish meat industry and the live exports trade; beef and cattle from the Republic are attractive because the Republic has a reputation for low BSE incidence, whereas in the UK there have already been more than 120,000 cases of BSE.

Meat processors in Northern Ireland are deeply concerned. The Chief Executive of the Northern Ireland Meat Exporters' Association has been quoted as saying: 'We are losing our raw material because of this trade. Agents from the Republic are in our livestock markets every week and they are certainly not buying to sell in Northern Ireland'.[44]

It is abundantly clear that the Irish trade in live animals is not without problems, and that Irish animals are suffering and dying as a result. Many people in the Republic of Ireland are becoming increasingly concerned about the inherent cruelty of transporting animals long distances only to face slaughter at their destination. Combined with the need to keep jobs in the meat processing industries in Ireland, there is a clear argument for slaughter at home and export of meat. In this way, responsibility for the welfare of Irish animals right up until their death remains in our own country and under our own control.

Part Three

The Way Forward

Chapter Fifteen

Need for the Live Trade to End

The suffering involved

Suffering is inherent in the long distance transport of animals. Animals are frequently given neither food nor water nor rest, even during journeys of 40 or 50 hours. This is particularly shocking when one bears in mind that after 10 hours without water cattle begin to dehydrate. Pigs can start to dehydrate after as little as 6 hours without water.[1]

Loading and unloading are especially stressful and the situation is often made worse by animals being pushed and beaten when they do not immediately move in the desired direction. In much of the EC electric goads are used on a regular basis.

Overcrowding is commonplace with animals crammed tightly into lorries with no regard for their space needs. It is worth quoting the European Commission on this point:

> The idea that animals should be packed into a vehicle as tightly as possible so that they support each other has been shown by experience and experiment to be fallacious. Animals are not like packing cases. They need a certain amount of space around them in order to move their limbs to brace themselves against the motion of the vehicle. They also need enough space to be able to get up if they fall, to avoid being trampled.[2]

P.V. Tarrant, a scientist researching the transportation of cattle by road, has written:

> The most common hazard on the moving vehicle is over-

loading, which greatly increases the risk of animal injury and damage to carcase and meat quality.[3]

He stresses that the greatest danger is irretrievable loss of balance with cattle going down underfoot. Once this happens there is a considerable risk of injury. This risk, he adds, is greatly increased by overcrowding.

Falling down is usually caused either by bad driving (rapid cornering or sudden braking) or strenuous and usually unsuccessful attempts to change position in a full pen. Once an animal falls in an overcrowded truck it may be trapped on the floor with dire consequences, such as being trampled on as other cattle close over it.[4]

The sheer stress of long journeys is highlighted by Tarrant's observation that at the end of 24 hour journeys cattle are very tired and lie down in the pens at the abattoir despite the unfamiliar surroundings and the nearness of strange cattle.

Tarrant concludes:

It is not unusual for transport conditions to deteriorate to an intolerable extent, causing animal suffering and economic losses.

A number of incidents described earlier show that the combination of high summer temperatures and poor ventilation can cause great distress and can lead to animals dying.

In 1993 new research showed that transport is extremely stressful for lambs.[5] Scientists, mainly from Bristol University, looked at one group of lambs who had been transported for 9 hours and another group transported for 14 hours.

They found that the lambs took a massive 144 hours (6 days) to recover 'almost completely'. They added that the lambs needed 96 hours (4 days) rest before being in an acceptable state to resume their journeys. It should be emphasised that these long recovery times were based on journeys of 9 and 14 hours. In reality, lambs are sometimes transported for 40 hours or more.

The researchers also reported that the average noise level during the journey was 90 db (A) and that the lambs were exposed to this level for a length of time that would be unacceptable to people.

Live trade should be replaced by carcase trade

Indeed, all this has been recognised by the European Commission, which in 1993 wrote:

Long distance transport in overstocked vehicles, combined with dehydration and starvation, results in very poor welfare and often in high mortality.[6]

For very many years Compassion in World Farming has argued that, as long as meat eating persists, animals should be sent to a slaughterhouse as near as possible to the farm on which they have been reared. The fresh meat can then be transported throughout the EU.

This view is shared by many bodies including the British Veterinary Association, Eurogroup for Animal Welfare and the RSPCA.

The Report of the European Scientific Veterinary Committee stressed that live transport 'should be avoided whenever possible'. They concluded that:

the occurrence of poor welfare can be reduced considerably by slaughtering near the point of rearing and transporting meat.[7]

The principle of slaughtering as near as possible to the farm is often translated into a call for an *overall* 8-hour journey limit. The European Parliament voted for such an 8-hour limit in 1990 and twice in 1993.

Compassion in World Farming believes that the time has come for a fundamental reappraisal of the trade. The trade in live animals should be stopped throughout the EU and be replaced by a carcase trade.

In the meantime, live exports from the UK should be halted as it is clear that once animals leave the UK the government is powerless to safeguard their welfare.

It should be emphasised that successive governments of all

parties have continued to obstruct welfare progress. Peter Roberts, Compassion in World Farming's founder, believes that the live trade is a blot on our culture comparable to the support we gave to the slave-trade. The export of animals for slaughter, whether immediately or after further fattening, should have been banned in favour of a carcase trade thirty years ago. Had this happened, the trend would have spread throughout Europe as it gathered respectability.

Need for tougher rules

Until the live trade ends, there is a need for stronger rules designed to minimise the suffering of the animals involved:

* Animals should be given food, water and rest at much more frequent intervals than those currently laid down by law.

* Maximum stocking densities must be established, based on the Scientific Veterinary Committee's principle that, with certain exceptions, animals must all be able to lie down at the same time.

* High standards of vehicle construction should be laid down, with certification of vehicles being compulsory.

* Training and licensing should be compulsory for drivers. Poor driving leads to corners being taken too fast and brakes applied too sharply. Tarrant writes that one-third of the cases where cattle are floored are caused by loss of balance during cornering.[8]

* There should be no exports to countries outside the EU which do not match EU welfare standards.

* The Commission's veterinary inspectorate must be given sufficient staff and resources to ensure effective enforcement. Member States must give enforcement a much higher priority within their territories.

Enforcement

A final word on enforcement. As we have seen, enforcement of the welfare rules is all but non-existent in many Member States. The Commission is supposed to ensure that Member States enforce EC laws in their territory. The full extent of the Commission's inactivity in this sphere was revealed when the Agriculture Commissioner, René Steichen, answered a Parliamentary Question from Anita Pollack MEP. He said that at present (1993) the Community has some twenty veterinary inspectors. These:

> are responsible for ensuring that Community veterinary regulations are applied in the Member States. [They are] also responsible for checking for compliance with the provisions on animal protection. However, the number of inspectors available is so small in relation to its field of activity that it has not yet been possible to make such checks.

So there we have it. By July 1993 the Commission had not managed to make one single check as to whether EC animal welfare laws were being complied with.

Nor did the position improve in 1994. Replying to a further Parliamentary Question, this time from Caroline Jackson MEP, the Commission stated that it had neither the funding nor the staff to monitor national compliance with the EU transport rules. It admitted that 'no checks have been made on compliance with Community rules on protection of animals during transport'.

Chapter Sixteen

The Status of Animals in the Treaty of Rome

One may ask why, given all the suffering involved, the European Community has not long ago brought the live trade to an end, allowing it to be replaced by a carcase trade.

Here we must approach the heart of the problem. The central principle of the Community is free trade. The Treaty of Rome (the cornerstone of European law) insists on the free movement of goods. This principle is believed in unquestioningly, with an almost religious fervour. To ask the committed Europhile to accept some restriction on free trade is rather like asking a true believer if they could just put this God business to one side.

Ah, well, you might say, that's all right, animals aren't goods. Oh yes they are. According to the Treaty of Rome they are.

And so we've arrived. At the heart of the problem.

The Treaty of Rome regards animals as 'goods' or 'products'. They are as much subject to the laws of free trade as television sets, cans of beer or meat.

Only if animals are given a new status in the Treaty can they be freed from the grip of the free trade laws.

All this was recognised in the late 80's by Peter Roberts, Compassion in World Farming's founder. He organised a petition calling for animals to be given a new status in the Treaty of Rome as 'sentient animals'.

The petition was eventually signed by over one million people from all 12 EC Member States. This achievement was thanks to the splendid efforts of Compassion in World

Farming's members and animal welfare societies throughout Europe.

The petition was the largest ever presented to the Parliament. It was formally presented on 13th March 1991 to the President of the European Parliament, Sr. Enrique Baron Crespo, by Joyce D'Silva (Compassion in World Farming's Director) accompanied by David Morris MEP (Labour) and Madron Seligman MEP (Conservative).

Joyce D'Silva had become Compassion in World Farming's Director on Peter Roberts' retirement. A scroll representing the one million signatures was presented by Joyce to Mary Banotti MEP, President of the Parliament's Intergroup on Animal Welfare. Over the years the Intergroup has done an enormous amount to secure improvements in animal welfare throughout Europe.

In documents accompanying the petition, Compassion in World Farming stated their belief that the relatively low priority given to farm animal welfare in EC legislation stems from the fact that the Treaty of Rome itself fails to give importance to, or provide a legal foundation for, animal welfare. This is illustrated by the classification of farm animals as agricultural products in Annex II to the Treaty. This places them in the same category as cereals and meat and fails to recognise the fact that they are living creatures.

To remedy this situation, Compassion in World Farming believes that the following Treaty changes are needed:

1 Animals should be given a new status as 'sentient animals' rather than as products.

2 A new Article should be added to the Treaty, similar to those on the environment introduced by the Single European Act in 1986. Articles 130 r-t give a status to environmental considerations and provide that action by the Community relating to the environment shall have the objective of protecting and improving its quality.

The new Article we seek would similarly give the welfare of animals a central place in the Treaty and should provide (as is the case with the environment) that animal welfare considerations shall be a component of the Community's other policies where relevant.

3 The welfare of animals should be established as one of the Community's central Principles (set out in Part One of the Treaty) governing policies and legislation which affect animals.

4 The welfare of farm animals should be added to paragraph 2 of Article 39, as one of the factors to be taken account of in working out the Common Agricultural Policy.

The petition received a quick response from the UK government which announced that the UK had proposed that the Inter-Governmental Conference (which was considering the 1991 round of changes to the Treaty of Rome) should make a declaration calling on the EC institutions 'to ensure that the Community, when taking any action which affects animals, pays full regard to their welfare requirements and their status as sentient beings'. Compassion in World Farming was delighted that the UK government had acknowledged that animals should be recognised as 'sentient beings'.

In due course a Declaration was added to the 1991 Maastricht Treaty, although at the insistence of France and Spain the reference to 'sentient beings' had to be dropped. The Declaration reads:

DECLARATION ON THE
PROTECTION OF ANIMALS

The Conference calls upon the European Parliament, the Council and the Commission, as well as Member States, when drafting and implementing Community legislation on the common agricultural policy, transport, the internal market and research, to pay full regard to the welfare requirements of animals.

In January 1994 Compassion in World Farming's petition came before the European Parliament which agreed with its principal demands and in particular that animals should be given a new status in the Treaty of Rome as sentient animals.

The Parliament's endorsement of the petition represents a major triumph. This, however, is not the end of the story as Treaty changes must be agreed by all the Member States of the European Union. The next round of Treaty changes is likely to be in 1996. Compassion in World Farming, together with other UK and European animal welfare societies, is already lobbying for the 1996 changes to give a new status to animals as demanded by the petition and the European Parliament.

This campaign received a considerable boost in the UK during the 1994 election campaign for the European Parliament. The Labour Party's manifesto called for animals to be given a new status in the Treaty of Rome as 'sentient beings' rather than agricultural products. In a document entitled 'Animal Welfare – The Conservative Record', the Conservatives referred to the Prime Minister's insistence on the inclusion in the Maastricht Treaty of the Declaration on the Protection of Animals. This Conservative Party document added that 'the Declaration is the first step towards the amendment of the Treaties, so that the protection of animals is fully incorporated among the recognised objectives of the European Union'. The Liberal Democrats stated that they would 'acknowledge animals as sentient beings capable of experiencing pain and suffering and argue for the promotion and protection of animals to be added to the EU Treaties as a function of the European Union'.

A new status for animals in the Treaty of Rome which recognised that they are neither 'goods' nor 'products' would bring immense benefits. In particular it would have an impact on the long distance transport of animals. As 'products' animals are subject to the Treaty's insistence on the free movement of goods.

If animals were no longer classified as products, it would prove easier to gain acceptance for the principle that the 'goods' in which there should be free trade are meat and meat products rather than live animals.

The author, Peter Stevenson, is the Political and Legal Director of Compassion in World Farming.

For information about Compassion in World Farming's campaigns against factory farming and the long distance transport of farm animals, please contact:

> **Compassion in World Farming**
> **Charles House**
> **5A Charles Street**
> **Petersfield**
> **Hampshire GU32 3EH**
> **Telephone: (0730) 264208/268863**

In the Republic of Ireland the address is: Compassion in World Farming, P.O. Box 206, Cork, Ireland.

In France, Compassion in World Farming's sister organisation is Protection Mondiale des Animaux de Ferme, Boite Postale 28, 72210 La Suze sur Sarthe, France.

Notes

Chapter One

1 Pamphlet published in 1957 by the Protection of Livestock for Slaughter Association.
2 The Report of the Balfour Committee of Enquiry published in April 1957. HMSO Reference No. CMND/154.

Chapter Two

1 RSPCA statement of intent on the export of food animals. 17th October 1972.
2 Letter dated 23rd July 1969 from Ministry of Agriculture, Fisheries & Food to Compassion in World Farming.
3 Ministry of Agriculture, Fisheries & Food Press Notice. 20th August 1970.
4 Ibid.
5 Report dated 29th October 1970 by the Deputy Chief Veterinary Officer of the RSPCA.

Chapter Three

1 Paper given by Mrs Eileen Bezet to Symposium held by the Animal Defence Society Limited on the Live Export of British Food Animals. 29th September 1972.
2 Daily Telegraph. 31st October 1970.
3 Eastern Daily Press. 30th October 1970.
4 As 2.
5 As 1.
6 Paper given by Mr John A Rixon, OBE, Director of Markets, City of Manchester, to Symposium on the Live Export of British Food Animals. 29th September 1972.
7 RSPCA statement of intent on the export of food animals. 17th October 1972.

8 As 6.
9 As 7.
10 *Sunday Times* Insight article. 23rd May 1971.
11 As 7.
12 As 1.
13 As 7.
14 Ibid.
15 *Farmers Weekly*. 11th June 1971.
16 Ibid.

Chapter Four

1 *News of the World*: 21st & 28th January 1973.
2 *News of the World*: 18th March 1973 and RSPCA Today: 1st March 1973.
3 Official Report. 12th July 1973. Vol. 859: Column 1837.
4 Official Report. 12th July 1973. Vol. 859: Column 1825.
5 *The Guardian*: 14th July 1973.
6 Reported in RSPCA Today: 1st March 1973.
7 *Farmers Guardian*: 8th February 1974.
8 Compassion in World Farming newsletter: 10th October 1973.
9 Quoted in *RSPCA Today*: 1st March 1973.
10 *Agscene* No. 26: April 1974.

Chapter Five

1 Report of the Committee on the Export of Animals for Slaughter, 27th March 1974. Cmnd 5566 (HMSO).
2 British Veterinary Association Press Statement. 27th March 1974.
3 Agscene No. 26: April 1974.
4 Ibid and RSPCA Press Release: 10th April 1974.
5 Ronald Atkins, MP. Official Report. 16th January 1975. Vol. 884: Column 773.
6 Quoted on BBC2: *Late News Extra*: 27th March 1974.
7 Mr McCall-Smith quoted by William Hamilton, MP. Official Report. 16th January 1975. Vol. 884: Column 768–769.
8 As 6.
9 Official Report. 16th January 1975. Vol. 884: Column 696.
10 Official Report. 16th January 1975. Vol. 884: Column 701.
11 Council Directive of 18th November 1974 on stunning of animals before slaughter (74/577/EEC).
12 *The British Farmer & Stockbreeder*. 24th April 1976.
13 *RSPCA Today*: 1st May 1974.
14 F.A. Burden, MP. Official Report. 16th January 1975. Vol. 884: Column 745.

15 European Convention for the protection of animals during international transport, 1967.
16 Report accompanying the Commission proposal for a Council Directive amending Directive 91/628/EEC on the protection of animals during transport (COM (93) 330 Final) submitted by the Commission on 26th August 1993.
17 Gwynfor Evans, MP. Official Report. 16th January 1975. Vol. 884: Column 735.
18 'The Editor's Diary' of the *Farmers Weekly*. Quoted by Miss Janet Fookes, MP. Official Report. 16th January 1975. Vol. 884: Column 755.

Chapter Six

1 *Agscene* No. 38. January 1976.
2 *Agscene* No. 47. November 1977.
3 *The Guardian*. 1st July 1977.
4 British Veterinary Association Press Statement. 30th June 1977.
5 'The export trade in live animals for slaughter or further fattening', a report by the Ministry of Food, the Department of Agriculture and Fisheries for Scotland and the Department of Agriculture for Northern Ireland. Published 23rd March 1978.
6 *Agscene* No. 47. November 1977.
7 *Daily Telegraph*. 12th September 1977.
8 Editor of the *Farmers Weekly* quoted in *Agscene* No. 47. November 1977.
9 *Agscene* No. 64. September 1981.
10. *Agscene* No. 67. May/June 1982.

Chapter Seven

1 Complaint to the Commission of the European Communities on the International Transport of Live Animals. RSPCA. February 1985.
2 *The Observer*. 16th October 1985.
3 *The Sunday Times*. 29th October 1989.

Chapter Eight

1 *The Daily Telegraph*. 31st July 1990.
2 *Wales on Sunday*: 26th August 1990 and *The Daily Telegraph*: 30th August 1990.
3 *Daily Mail*. 24th August 1990.
4 *The Times*. 30th August 1990.
5 *The Daily Telegraph*. 30th August 1990.

6 *The Times.* 7th September 1990.
7 *The Daily Telegraph.* 7th September 1990.
8 *The Daily Telegraph.* 13th September 1990.
9 *The Times.* 27th September 1990.
10 *Daily Express.* 10th September 1990.
11 *The European.* 14th September 1990.
12 *The Independent.* 14th September 1990.
13 R. v. Minister of Agriculture, Fisheries and Food ex parte Peter Roberts [1991] 1. C.M.L.R. 555.
14 *Agscene* No. 105. Winter 1991.

Chapter Nine

1 Report of the Working Group 'Transport of Farm Animals and Pets' of the Scientific Veterinary Committee, Section: Animal Welfare. Brussels. 30th April 1992.
2 Proposal for a Council Directive amending Directive 91/628/EEC on the protection of animals during transport. (COM (93) 330 Final). Submitted by the Commission on 26th August 1993.

Chapter Ten

1 The Welfare of Calves Regulations 1987.
2 'Hook versus hoof. The drive behind the increasing shipment of live lambs to the Continent.' RSPCA. November 1993.
3 *Meat Trades Journal.* 27th May 1993.
4 Webster, J., Saville, C. and Welchman D. Improved husbandry systems for veal calves. Published by the Animal Health Trust and the Farm Animal Care Trust.
5 D.P.P. v. Henn & Darby [1980] 2. C.M.L.R. 229.
6 Council Directive of 19th November 1991 laying down minimum standards for the protection of calves (91/629/EEC).
7 Anita Groener v. The Minister for Education and City of Dublin Vocational Education Committee [1990]. 1. C.M.L.R. 401.
8 Trunkfield H.R. and Broom D.M. The welfare of calves during handling and transport. Applied Animal Behaviour *Science* 28 (1990) 135–152.
9 Ibid.
10 Staples G.E. and Haugse L.N., 1974. Losses in young calves after transportation. *British Veterinary Journal,* 130: 374–378.
11 Barnes M.A., Carter R.E., Longnecker J.V., Riesen J.W. and Woody C.O. 1975. Age at transport and calf survival. *Journal of Dairy Science* 58: 1247.

Chapter Eleven

1 Report of the Working Group 'Transport of Farm Animals and Pets' of the Scientific Veterinary Committee, Section: Animal Welfare. Brussels. 30th April 1992.
2 Report accompanying Commission proposal for a Council Directive amending Directive 91/628/EEC on the protection of animals during transport. August 1993.
3. Eurogroup Report. Dossier to the UK Presidency of the European Community 'Farm animals sent for slaughter across Europe'. 9th July 1992.
4 As 1.
5 *Scottish Farmer*. 26th February 1994.
6 Eurostat – Comext 1992.

Chapter Twelve

1 Nigel James of Welsh Store Stock quoted in *Agscene* No. 97. November/December 1989.
2 *European AgriBusiness*. February 1993.
3 *Le Provencal*. 30th July 1993.
4 'An economic comparison of alternative methods of exporting beef and sheep meat from the UK'. Professor Christopher Ritson.
5 'Hook versus hoof. The drive behind the increasing shipment of live lambs to the Continent.' RSPCA. November 1993.
6 Ibid.
7 Ibid and RSPCA press release of 3rd November 1993.
8 *Scottish Farmer*. 15th January 1994.
9 *Farmers Weekly*. 16th July 1993.
10 *Green Europe*. March 1992.
11 *European AgriBusiness*. June 1993.
12 *European AgriBusiness*. January 1993.
13 *Meat Trades Journal*. 8th July 1993.
14 *Meat Trades Journal*. 27th May 1993.
15 *Farmers Guardian*. 28th May 1993.
16 *Meat Trades Journal*. 24th June 1993.
17 Ibid.
18 *European AgriBusiness*. May 1993.
19 *Meat Trades Journal*. 24th June 1993.
20 As 5.
21 *European AgriBusiness*. March 1994.
22 *European AgriBusiness*. September 1993.
23 *Meat Trades Journal*. 26th August 1993.
24 Richard Cracknell of ABP quoted in *Meat Trades Journal*. 26th August 1993.

25 *Meat Trades Journal*. 3rd February 1994.
26 *Farmers Guardian*. 24th December 1993.
27 *Meat Trades Journal* Editorial. 22nd July 1993.
28 'Soames attacked over meat export comments.' *Meat Trades Journal*. 22nd July 1993.

Chapter Thirteen

1 Ministry of Agriculture News Release. 4th November 1993.
2 *Farming News*. 'Live exports bring foot-and-mouth risk'. 5th November 1993.
3 Parliamentary answer by the Minister of Agriculture, the Rt. Hon. Gillian Shephard MP. Official Record. 25th November 1993: Columns 120–121.
4 *Farming News*. 'Live imports are a much greater worry'. 5th November 1993.
5 Official Report. 13th May 1994. Columns 291–292.
6 Ministry of Agriculture News Release. 15th February 1994.
7 As 6, and Radio 4's *Farming Today* on 18th February 1994.
8 Birmingham City Council Press Release. 9th March 1994.
9 *Farming News*. 18th March 1994.
10 Birmingham City Council Press Release. 11th March 1994.
11 Birmingham City Council Press Releases. 10th & 11th March 1994.
12 Birmingham City Council Press Release. 17th March 1994.
13 As 12.
14 Official Report. 18th April 1994. Columns 412–413.
15 *Farmers Weekly*. 25th February 1994.
16 Official Report. 6th May 1994. Column 697.
17 *Sunday Business Post*, 17th April 1994 and The Observer, 1st May 1994.
18 Official Report. 3rd May 1994. Columns 480–481.
19 Official Report. 2nd March 1994. Column 742.

Chapter Fourteen

1 1993 Annual Review and Outlook for Agriculture, the Food Industry, and Forestry. Department of Agriculture, Food and Forestry. Dublin, 1993.
2 1993 Annual Review and Outlook. CBF (Irish Livestock and Meat Board). Dublin, 1993.
3 1988 Annual Review and Outlook. CBF (Irish Livestock and Meat Board). Dublin, 1988.
4 As 2.
5 1992 Annual statistics for exports of live animals, Central Statistics Office. Dublin, 1992.

6 As 2.

7 1992 Annual Review and Outlook. CBF (Irish Livestock and Meat Board). Dublin, 1992.

8 As 5.

9 *Scottish Farmer*. 4th December 1993.

10 Personal communication with cattle farmer, 1993.

11 As 2.

12 As 2.

13 Personal communication, M.A. Bartlett and Department of Agriculture, Food and Forestry. 10th March 1994.

14 *Irish Times*. 10th March 1994.

15 Letter from Department of Agriculture, Food and Forestry to Compassion in World Farming, Ireland. 6th April 1994.

16 *Cork Examiner*. 4th September 1992.

17 *Sunday Times*. 4th July 1993.

18 Ibid.

19 *Readers Digest*. April 1994.

20 As 13.

21 Report of Inspector of the Cork Society for the Prevention of Cruelty to Animals. 20th December 1979.

22 Letter from A. Dukes (then Minister of Agriculture) to J. O'Keeffe TD. 12th January 1982.

23 *Sunday Tribune*. 18th April 1982.

24 *Irish Times*. 20th January 1992.

25 *Agscene*. Spring 1990.

26 *Irish Times*. 9th October 1975.

27 *Herald Express*. 18th and 20th December 1993.

28 *Irish Times*. 20th January 1992.

29 *Sunday Business Post*. 14th February 1993.

30 *Irish Times*. 15th November 1993.

31 Economic interpretations of the history of Waterford. A. Downey. 1932.

32 *Cork Examiner*. 28th April 1994.

33 *Cork Examiner*. 14th August 1993.

34 *Irish Independent*. 10th May 1994.

35 *Meat Trades Journal*. 26th May 1994.

36 *Irish Farmers Journal*. 23rd April 1994.

37 *The Observer*. 1st May 1994.

38 *Irish Times*. 10th March 1994.

39 *Irish Farmers Journal*. 12th March 1994.

40 *Sunday Business Post*. 17th April 1994.

41 *European Agribusiness*, April 1994 and The Scottish Farmer, 2nd April 1994.

42 *European Agribusiness*, April 1994 and The Times, 23rd April 1994.

43 *The Times*. 23rd April 1994.
44 Ibid.

Chapter Fifteen

1 Report of the Working Group, 'Transport of Farm Animals and Pets' of the Scientific Veterinary Committee, Section: Animal Welfare. Brussels, 30th April 1992.
2 Report accompanying the Commission proposal for a Council Directive amending Directive 91/628/EEC on the protection of animals during transport. August 1993.
3 Tarrant, P.V. Transportation of cattle by road. *Applied Animal Behaviour Science*, 28 (1990) 153–170.
4 Ibid.
5 Knowles T.G., Warris P.D., Brown S.N., Kestin S.C., Rhind S.M., Edwards J.E., Anil M.H. and Dolan S.K., 1993. Long distance transport of lambs and the time needed for subsequent recovery. Veterinary Record 133: 286–293.
6 As 2.
7 As 1.
8 As 3.